Enjoying Microwave Cooking
Discovering Delicious Recipes

BY JANET L. SADLACK

Contents

Pictured on Cover: Corn and Beef-Stuffed Peppers, page 36, Fruit and Cream Sparkle, page 71, and Easy Cheesy French Fries, page 56.

Recipes Unlimited, Inc. specializes in developing cook books and other related recipe materials for manufacturers and consumers. Although the company has developed several microwave cook books for major manufacturers, this is the first cook book marketed under the Recipes Unlimited name.

Janet L. Jones Sadlack is a home economics graduate from Oregon State University. Prior to establishing Recipes Unlimited, she was responsible for cook book development for The Pillsbury Company, and later served as a cook book consultant for several microwave companies, equipment manufacturers and food companies. For several years, she taught microwave cooking classes through a local adult education program.

The recipes in this book were tested in 600 to 650-watt countertop microwave ovens. For other types of ovens, some adjustment in cooking times may be necessary to achieve the doneness described in the recipes. *Unless a lower power setting is specified in the recipe, use high or "cook" setting.*

Recipes Unlimited also publishes a bi-monthly publication especially for microwave oven owners, "The Microwave Times." Subscription price: $4.95 for one year (6 issues), $8.95 for two years (12 issues).

ISBN: 0-918620-01-5 — soft cover
ISBN: 0-918620-02-3 — hard cover

Dear Friend,

During the past nine years I have been discovering and enjoying the flexibility and new freedom a microwave oven adds to one's lifestyle.

These experiences have come from successes and failures in my home kitchen, from teaching microwave cooking classes, and through Recipes Unlimited in the projects we do for microwave oven manufacturers in our test kitchen.

I remember my first days with the oven and the awesome feeling from such a precise timer, so many things to do and not to do, and the total newness of this unique way of cooking. With time, though, I soon realized that while microwave cooking is new and different, much of what occurs also happens when cooking on a burner or in a regular oven. It just happens faster.

Most of us grow up with cooking an integral part of our lives and we take much of it for granted without giving much thought to the whys and hows. With microwave cooking, we are confronted with a new cooking experience all at once when the oven arrives, and many times feel we should learn it just about as quickly. But whether you learn it in a day or two or during a year or two, the important thing is that the oven adapts to and compliments your own lifestyle.

Personally, I enjoy using the microwave oven along with other cooking appliances. But for you, the type of usage may be quite different. It will develop as you understand and use the oven in ways that are enjoyable and satisfying to you. That is what this book is all about — understanding microwave cooking and enjoying it within your own cooking pattern.

Some of the cooking methods presented here are similar to those recommended by your oven manufacturer; others may differ. Oven features also vary and with some of the recipes you will find directions for using them. In addition, instructions are included for preparing the food without the use of the feature. For maximum use of your oven, experiment with various methods and features as they suit your circumstances to find the ones you prefer.

A number of former students have participated in the development of this book. In addition to the ideas and questions stimulated in classes, several students have tested and evaluated the recipes in their own homes. Their comments and suggestions have been most valuable and to assist you, some are included with the recipes.

We at Recipes Unlimited hope this book adds to your own enjoyment and understanding of microwave cooking as you discover its many delicious recipes.

Sincerely,

Janet L. Sadlack

Janet L. Sadlack
Recipes Unlimited, Inc.
Box 1202
Burnsville, Minnesota 55337

Learning
Microwave Cooking

Microwave cooking is indeed an exciting new way of cooking. For some new oven owners, it is readily an exciting and enjoyable learning experience. For others, the fast-cooking, space-age appliance may present a challenge within the once secure and familiar kitchen. The comments on this page reflect common learning experiences to provide added encouragement for you.

When learning microwave cooking methods, begin with simple foods that cook or heat in familiar ways. Heat rolls or bread items, reheat leftovers, soften butter, heat water and milk and cook vegetables, sauces and puddings. Then, as you feel at ease with these foods, try others where there is some change, but where the results are still quite familiar. Experiment with some casseroles, a meat loaf or some fish, some chicken recipes, a frozen pie and an egg recipe or two. Then, when you feel familiar with these, prepare some of the foods that are different because they lack a crust or browning. These include cakes, cookies, breads and other baked items.

As you try various types of foods, there will be some you like to prepare exclusively in the microwave oven, others that you wish to prepare only occasionally by microwaves and still others that you prefer to prepare in your regular oven or on a burner. Sometimes a preference is based on speed or the advantage of cooking in a serving dish. Other times it is a superior end product or it saves heating up the oven, and at times it only reflects the way you feel. Just don't think that you should prepare everything in the microwave oven! You do have other types of cooking equipment available and they should continue to serve a useful purpose right along with the microwave oven.

As you are learning microwave cooking, don't become a "slave" to the appliance. You may find yourself running to set the table or rushing to prepare the other foods by the time the food in the microwave oven is ready. However, this isn't necessary. If you do get behind, just let the microwave cooked food sit. Then, when everything else is ready, check to see if it is still hot enough to serve. If it is not, just microwave a minute or two until it is piping hot once again. Only you will know that it has been ready for 15 minutes!

At first you may feel insecure using the new oven since it is necessary to refer continually to recipes and time charts until the techniques and methods become familiar. This probably seems like a real nuisance when you have been preparing day-to-day meals for your family for years without referring to guides. However, if you try just one recipe per meal and understand the "whys" of the techniques, it will not be long until you will be using your microwave oven without constant reference to a book.

Learning anything is often more enjoyable when the experience is shared with someone else. If you have a friend or neighbor who shares your interest in microwave cooking, you may want to get together on a regular basis. Each time you meet, try a new recipe from this or another favorite book and share your experiences. Or, investigate microwave cooking classes in your area. There is nothing better than a little encouragement when you're learning something new.

So, although learning microwave cooking is a new experience, it need not be an insurmountable challenge. Just go about it at your own speed and interest level. Relax while the oven works for you to add flexibility and enjoyment to your meal preparation.

The Cooking Process

The heat that results from cooking with your regular range comes from an external source — either a hot burner or the oven cavity which transfers the heat into the cooking container and then the food. Microwave cooking is different because the heat originates within the food.

This section provides the background information on how this happens and what it accomplishes. The recipes throughout the book automatically take this information into consideration, but if you wish to change or alter a recipe, an understanding of the microwave cooking process is essential.

MICROWAVES

Microwave cooking requires that electricity be converted into microwaves through a magnetron tube inside the oven. These microwaves pass through a channel into the oven cavity where they are usually distributed by a fan or stirrer. As they move about within the oven, the microwaves are absorbed by the food. The moisture molecules within the food are agitated at a tremendous rate, and this agitation creates heat within the food.

This type of cooking is often faster and more efficient since only the food is heated. Any heat noticed inside the oven or from the baking dishes comes from the food as it becomes hot.

Place foods in the oven so that microwaves can easily reach all parts. Place one item in the center,

two items on each side of the center, three items at the points of a triangle, four items at the points of a square and five items in a circle.

POWER LEVELS

Many microwave ovens have a selection of lower power settings. These settings reduce the microwave energy available, allowing foods to cook more slowly. The result often means less chance of overcooking the edges and minimal attention required to rotate and stir the food during the cooking process.

If your oven does not have a lower power setting (even a defrost button is lower power), you can often achieve similar results by allowing occasional standing times during the cooking steps.

The recipes in this book include lower power timings (we call it variable power) and directions in some recipes and many of the TIPS. Thus, you can select the faster cooking "high" power method or the more leisurely "variable power" method.

Since terminology for variable power settings varies with manufacturer and oven models, there is a convenient chart on the inside back cover to show how our variable power settings relate to the particular oven you may be using.

BROWNING ELEMENTS

Some microwaves have a calrod unit in the top of the oven that can be used to achieve drying and some browning of food surfaces. Usually, the browning feature is used following the microwave cooking. Distance from the element is important to the timing. If your particular oven does not have a shelf position that allows for the correct placement, use an overturned casserole or sauce dish to achieve the desired distance from the browning element.

Additional browning is also possible by placing the food under the broiler in the conventional oven. Watch foods closely since the broiler element is more intense and will usually brown more quickly.

USES

The microwave oven produces instant heat within foods, but many times this only penetrates a portion of the food. The heating of the remainder of the food relies on the transfer of heat. This is true with any of the three uses of the microwave oven: defrosting, heating or cooking.

When **DEFROSTING**, the microwaves change ice to water. This process needs to happen slowly so the food does not become hot and begin to cook. With many items, standing times are necessary during the defrosting.

When **HEATING**, the already cooked food becomes hot, but does not change in texture or appearance. Porous items heat through very quickly. More dense items need stirring, rearranging or standing to heat the center without overheating the edges.

COOKING involves sustained heating so the food can change in texture, consistency, appearance and/or flavor. With quick-cooking foods, the desired doneness can be achieved quite easily in the microwave oven. However, with longer cooking foods, it is often easier to use a source of heat where the cooking can be controlled and slowed more easily.

The results desired — defrosting, heating or cooking — help determine the time and techniques necessary.

FACTORS WHICH INFLUENCE COOKING TIME

VOLUME: The more items or the larger the quantity of food, the longer the defrosting, heating or cooking time. With one potato in the oven, all the available microwaves are used for cooking it alone. But, when two other potatoes are added, the one potato must share the available microwaves with the others. When *heating* items, the increase in time is proportional to the increase in volume. For example, 1 cup of water heats in about 1 minute and 2 cups heat in about 2 minutes. When *cooking* is involved, the increase varies according to the food. Some foods cook just about as quickly as they are heated, and with these foods the increase in time is proportional to the increase in volume. Other foods must remain at a heated temperature for a period of time before they are considered cooked. With these foods, the time increase is usually ½ to ¾ the increase in quantity.

STARTING TEMPERATURE: The colder an item, the longer it will take to heat. A refrigerated item requires more time to heat than the same item at room temperature. Or, a frozen item takes longer than the same item at a refrigerated temperature.

DENSITY: The more dense an item, the longer it takes for microwaves to penetrate throughout. Density and its importance in microwave cooking is the reason why it is *not* possible to say, "always heat one cup of a mixture for one minute". Instructions can only call for heating one cup of a porous mixture ¼ to ½ minute, and heating one cup of a more dense mixture 1 to 2 minutes. With porous items, the microwaves readily penetrate throughout and agitate the moisture molecules. With denser items, they only penetrate the outer portion and agitate these molecules. The inner portion heats as this heat is transferred into the center. With items where the heat takes longer to reach the center, it may be necessary to use a standing time or lower power setting to allow the heat to reach the center without overcooking the edges. Density is important when defrosting, heating and cooking.

FAT AND SUGAR CONTENT: Items high in either sugar or fat will heat more quickly than items low in these ingredients. Since these ingredients attract microwaves, the sugary filling of a sweet roll will heat more quickly than the bread portion. Or, the fat portion of a meat slice will heat more quickly than the remainder.

TECHNIQUES WHICH INFLUENCE COOKING TIME

ARRANGEMENT: Arrangement can be used to help even the defrosting, heating or cooking of foods. Since the microwaves penetrate the outer portion of food, arrange the food so the denser, thicker areas are near the edge and the thinner or more porous items or areas are near the center. Or, just eliminate the center by forming a "ring" shape.

When arranging leftovers on a plate, place the thick pieces toward the rim of the plate and the thin pieces toward the center. With dense items, like potatoes, spread them slightly and make an indentation in the center.

STIRRING: Stirring or rearranging is also used to help even the defrosting, heating or cooking of foods. Whenever it is possible to stir an item and there is a possibility that the outside will heat faster, stirring is a very effective means to achieve even cooking.

STANDING TIME: When arrangement or stirring will not even the cooking adequately, just turn off the oven and let the food stand a few minutes. This allows the heat at the outside of the food to penetrate the center without continued cooking on the outside. Standing time is also a factor at the end of cooking. Food coming from a microwave oven is similar to food removed from a burner with a high setting. It continues to bubble and cook. The hotter the food and more dense the item, the longer it will hold the heat and continue to cook after removal from the oven.

ROTATING: Different areas of a food cook at varying rates. By occasionally turning the dish with the food, it is possible to even the cooking. This is often recommended with casseroles and meats that are not stirred or rearranged and with breads, cakes, cookies and pies.

COVERINGS

A covering is used on a cooking dish to hold in the heat and speed the defrosting, heating or cooking. For some foods the covering should be tight fitting. For others, it should allow the moisture to escape. Occasionally a covering is used primarily to prevent spattering.

TIGHT-FITTING COVERS: This type of cover can include a casserole cover, an overturned plate or baking dish and plastic wrap. They can be used interchangeably, but use the plastic wrap only if it will not be touching the food. As the food becomes hot, the plastic may soften or melt when it is in contact with food. Tight-fitting covers are used on foods that are simmered, steamed or otherwise kept moist. Be careful when removing these coverings because the container is filled with hot steam.

SEMI-TIGHT COVERS: Waxed paper is often used when this type of cover is desired. When laid across the top of a casserole or dish, it fits fairly tightly, yet some steam can escape. This holds in the heat, yet allows browning to take place. It is often used with meat items where browning is desired along with steaming.

A waxed paper tent on roast poultry or meat helps retain the heat and prevents spattering.

LOOSE-FITTING COVERS: These include covers that readily allow moisture to pass through. Paper towels or napkins are examples and are often used with bread items and crumb toppings, allowing the moisture to readily evaporate. They are also helpful when it is desirable to evaporate excess moisture.

Selecting Utensils

When microwaves come in contact with a substance, they are **ABSORBED, REFLECTED** or **TRANSFERRED**. Cooking utensils used in the oven are selected according to their capacity to interact with microwaves. Most utensils should transfer the microwaves so that they do not interfere with the cooking process.

FOODS ABSORB MICROWAVES.

When food absorbs microwaves, it becomes hot. Most cooking utensils do not absorb microwaves. Wood and straw are usually not recommended for microwave cooking because they can contain moisture and will become hot. With continued use, they can dry to the point of cracking.

METAL REFLECTS MICROWAVES.

The walls of the oven are made of metal so the microwaves are reflected and retained within the oven cavity. Metal cooking containers are not recommended because the microwaves cannot reach the food in areas surrounded by metal.

Some oven manufacturers recommend never using metal in the oven, while others state that occasional use will not harm the oven. If you elect to use metal, only use it when it serves a real purpose and always be sure there is ample food (at least 2 cups) in the oven at the time. With this amount of food in the oven, the microwaves are attracted primarily to the moisture-bearing food item, and the metal only disrupts the cooking pattern slightly.

When there is little or no food in the oven, small pieces of metal can act like antennas and cause "arcing". This creates a sparkling, lightning-like effect and you can hear it as well as see the sparks when near the oven. These sparks will set paper or plastic on fire. Thus, be especially careful of metal twist-ties, since the metal is often surrounded by paper or plastic and will readily burn when arcing occurs. A rubber band or string rather than a twist-tie should be used to hold a plastic bag closed. Arcing may also occur when a metallic-trimmed dish is used

that contains very little food. It only takes a few seconds of arcing to ruin a dish. So guard against using dishes with gold or silver trim and designs, especially when heating a small amount of food. Large metal pieces like baking pans do not normally cause arcing, they just prevent efficient cooking. But, small pieces of metal combined with a small amount of food can produce arcing.

Metal in the form of aluminum foil can be used to advantage when you wish to prevent or slow the defrosting, cooking or heating of an area. If you wish to thaw only half a package of meat, wrap the one half in foil and it will remain frozen while the other half defrosts. Or, if a portion of a roast or other food item is cooking too fast, place a small piece of foil over the area you wish to cook more slowly. Since the metal reflects the microwaves, they will not reach this part of the food, and since there is plenty of food, no arcing will result. Be sure when thawing frozen juices or fruits that the container is not foil-lined. If it is, at least remove the top so the microwaves can enter from one side. This also applies to softening butter or cream cheese wrapped in foil-type paper.

Foil is used on poultry and meats to protect thin areas from overcooking.

GLASS, PLASTIC AND PAPER TRANSFER MICROWAVES. Most GLASSWARE is excellent for use in the microwave oven because the microwaves can readily pass through it into the food. The glass may be in the form of a serving dish or plate, a storage jar or measuring cup or a baking dish or casserole.

The type of glass is not a factor when *heating* or *defosting.* However, it is important when *cooking* foods that will be in contact with the glass for a period of time. Oven-proof baking dishes and casseroles are best for this type of cooking. When a recipe is to be baked or broiled in addition to microwave cooking, an oven-proof dish should definitely be used. Pyroceramic dishes are oven-proof and also designed to be used on a burner. They are convenient when it is necessary to prebrown or simmer a food along with microwave cooking.

Pottery makes a convenient cooking and serving dish. Most types are usable in the microwave oven, but occasionally pottery has a glaze that contains a substance which attracts microwaves. If this is the case, the food will cook much more slowly than the recipe indicates.

GLASS TEST: If you wonder about the suitability or usability of a piece of glassware or pottery, place it in the oven along with about 1 cup of water in a glass cup. Microwave ¼ to ½ minute. If the glassware has not become warm, it can be used in the oven. (The cup with the water may be warm, but only because the warm water has made it warm.) If the glassware feels warm or hot, it is best not to use it in the oven as it will absorb some of the microwaves. Not only will it slow the cooking of the food items, repeated usage can damage the dish.

PLASTIC also transfers microwaves. Most dishwasher-safe plastics are usable in the microwave oven for *defrosting* or *heating.* For *cooking,* specially designed plastic utensils as well as cooking bags and pouches will hold their shape during the continued exposure to the hot food. Plastic microwave utensils vary in heat resistency. Some are designed only for microwaving while others will also withstand conventional oven temperatures. Plastic wrap can be used as a covering for cooking or heating when it will not have contact with the food. On frozen items, plastic wrapping can be left on until the item is partially defrosted. When the item is rearranged or separated into pieces, the plastic covering can be removed.

PAPER products transfer microwaves and are convenient when heating many items. Since they absorb moisture and fat, they are often used when heating bread products or for cooking bacon. Frozen items packaged in paper can often remain in the package for defrosting or heating. If the package is overwrapped with waxed paper, place the package on a paper towel so the ink will not melt onto the oven surface.

Now you can cook pudding in a measuring cup, heat ice cream topping in the jar, and cook vegetables in the paper or plastic packaging.

PROBES AND THERMOMETERS
Many ovens are equipped with temperature probes which sense the internal temperature of a food and automatically shut off the oven when the preset desired temperature is reached. It is important to insert the probe into the food at an almost horizontal position. Also, the food should be firm enough to hold the probe in a constant position and to surround it evenly.

Special microwave thermometers are available that register the internal temperature of a food. As with the probe, there should be ample food surrounding the thermometer to achieve an accurate reading. Ordinary meat or candy thermometers should not be used during microwave cooking since the microwaves can cause damage and inaccuracy.

Defrosting Foods

ABOUT DEFROSTING: The time and technique necessary for defrosting depend upon the density of the food.

Porous items like breads, cakes or pies defrost throughout quite quickly. More dense items like meats and casseroles, defrost quickly on the outside, but require longer for the center to defrost. With these foods, lower power settings or standing times are necessary to allow the center to defrost without cooking the outside portion.

The ideal power level for defrosting keeps enough heat in the edges to warm and thaw the frozen center portion, yet not enough to start cooking. When cooking is noticed, the power level should be decreased so there will be less microwaving and potential cooking.

Some ovens have a defrost feature which automatically turns the oven on and off to provide microwave and stand timings. With most of these ovens, the timer is set for the total microwave and stand times even though microwave cooking is taking place only half the time. The defrost feature is convenient to use with dense items such as meats and casseroles that require periodic stand times. Meats weighing 1 to 2 lbs. defrost very easily with just the defrost feature. Larger cuts of meat will probably also require a few extra standing times as well as an occasional turn. More porous items usually defrost so quickly that standing times are not necessary and so the defrost feature is not used.

Some manufacturers have the defrost setting at about ⅓ normal power (30%) while others use a setting that equals about ½ power (50%). With smaller quantities, the ⅓ power level is most effective while with larger amounts the ½ power setting is more efficient.

DEFROSTING REMINDERS

• If cooking is noticed, lower the power setting to slow the process.

• When possible, separate or rearrange pieces about halfway through defrosting time. Once a portion is thawed, it can be removed from the oven while the remainder defrosts.

• Leave foods wrapped in paper or plastic until ready to separate or rearrange the food. This retains the heat and helps the center to thaw more quickly.

Use this chart as a guide for defrosting meat-type items. With larger quantities, some standing time is advisable once the edges of the food become warm. Normally, this is about ⅔ of the way through the defrosting process. Where several standing times are suggested, space them evenly during the last half of the defrosting time. Occasionally turning the item over helps even the defrosting.

DEFROSTING MEAT, FISH AND POULTRY

Amount	Time	Setting
½ lb.	2 to 3 minutes	low — 30%
1 lb.	5 to 6 minutes	low — 30%
2 lbs.	9 to 11 minutes	low — 30%
3 lbs.	14 to 16 minutes	med. — 50%
5 lbs.	20 to 25 minutes allow one standing time	med. — 50%
7 lbs.	30 to 35 minutes allow two standing times	med. — 50%
10 lbs.	45 to 50 minutes allow three standing times	med. — 50%
15 lbs.	55 to 60 minutes allow three standing times	med. — 50%
20 lbs.	75 to 80 minutes allow four standing times	med. — 50%

TIPS • Allow the food to stand at the end of the microwave time for a period about equal to the defrosting time. If additional defrosting is necessary, continue microwaving for a few minutes at the same reduced power setting.

• With Full Power, use the above timings as an overall guide. Have the microwave on for about ⅓ of the time for the low setting and about ½ the time for the medium setting.

Heating Foods

ABOUT HEATING: Foods reheat beautifully in the microwave oven. Leftovers taste as good as when freshly prepared, and it is no longer necessary to keep foods hot until everyone has eaten. Just set the food aside for the latecomers, and then reheat when they are ready to eat. Density is the primary influence on heating times, but sugar and fat content also play a role. As long as a distinction is made between dense and porous items, general heating guidelines can be used. Porous items and foods high in fat or sugar heat very quickly while denser items will require longer to heat. As an example of the influence sugar has on heating time, 1 cup of syrup heats in about ½ minute, but 1 cup of water will require about 1 minute to reach the same temperature. Sugar and fat mixtures attract microwaves, allowing them to absorb most of the available microwaves.

Since heating requires that microwaves only penetrate the food and create heat within, heating time extensions are usually proportional to increases in quantity. Only as you heat large quantities in a single container will you notice a heating time increase a little greater than the quantity increase.

Individual items heat more quickly than the same quantity in one container. For example, 3 cups of water heat in about 3 minutes, but 3 cups of water in one dish require about 4 minutes to heat.

For even heating, keep food pieces of uniform size and thickness, arrange thicker, more dense pieces toward the outside, and cover, stir or rearrange as necessary.

Many ovens have a reheat setting which is slightly slower than the regular high setting. When using a reheat setting, timings will be near the maximum suggested.

HEATING REMINDERS
• Allow 1 to 2 minutes for each cup of dense foods. Decrease time slightly when food is high in fat or sugar.
• Allow about ¼ minute for each serving of porous foods. Decrease time slightly when food is high in fat or sugar.
• Heating time increases proportionately to increases in quantity.
• Cover, rearrange or stir dense items to speed and even the heating. When this is not possible, switch to a lower setting (about ⅔ power) once the edges are hot. Or, allow the food to stand a few minutes during the heating time.

Use these times as guides for heating breads, rolls, cakes and pies.

HEATING POROUS ITEMS

Amount	Microwave Time
1 serving - about	¼ minute
2 servings - ¼ to	½ minute
3 servings - ½ to	¾ minute
4 servings - ¾ to	1 minute
6 servings - 1 to	1½ minutes

Use these times as guides for heating beverages, soups and casseroles.

HEATING DENSE ITEMS

Amount	Microwave Time
1 cup	1 to 2 minutes
2 cups -	2 to 3 minutes
3 cups -	3 to 4 minutes
4 cups -	4 to 5 minutes
6 cups -	6 to 8 minutes

Because of the fat content and thin slices or pieces, meats require less heating time than other dense items.

HEATING MEAT, POULTRY AND FISH

Amount	Microwave Time
1 serving -	½ to 1 minute
2 servings -	1 to 1½ minutes
3 servings -	1½ to 2 minutes
4 servings -	2 to 2½ minutes
6 servings -	3 to 3½ minutes
8 servings -	4 to 5 minutes

Fish and Seafood

ABOUT FISH AND SEAFOOD:
Steamed and poached fish dishes cook beautifully in the microwave oven. The fish cooks quickly and if not overcooked, will have a pleasant, mild flavor. Since it does cook rapidly, little browning can be expected. Several recipes include special coatings and toppings to add an attractive color.

Fish cooks in about the same time it requires to become hot. Usually the pieces are cut thinly enough to allow the microwaves to readily penetrate throughout. For fillets and thinly-cut steaks, allow about 4 minutes cooking time per lb. of fish. Cook until it can just be flaked apart easily with a fork. Then allow to stand covered a minute or two to finish cooking. Be careful about overcooking fish, as this gives a dry texture and strong flavor.

To speed the cooking, a covering is normally used. Plastic wrap, waxed paper and casserole covers can be used interchangeably. All hold in the steam and speed the cooking. Leave fish uncovered only when there is a topping or coating on the fish that you wish to remain crisp. Even here, a covering of paper toweling is often desirable.

Small pieces of frozen fish, like shrimp, can be thawed and cooked at the same time. Larger pieces, like lobster tails and fillets, are best thawed before cooking.

Pictured, top to bottom: Salmon Steaks with Cucumber Sauce, this page, Fillets Almondine, page 15, and Oriental Shrimp and Vegetables, page 17.

FISH AND SEAFOOD REMINDERS
• Allow 4 minutes per lb. cooking time for fillets and thinly-cut fish steaks.
• Cook fish covered, if possible.
• Be careful not to overcook fish — it should just flake apart easily with a fork. Allow to stand a few minutes before serving.
• Cook fish just before planning to serve. It does not reheat as well as other foods and there is a chance of overcooking when reheating.
• If browning is desirable, place cooked fish under the preheated broiler for a minute or two. Or, use the browning element if your oven is so equipped.

Poached salmon steaks topped with a sour cream and cucumber sauce. Pictured on page 12.

SALMON STEAKS WITH CUCUMBER SAUCE

    4 salmon steaks, cut 1-inch thick (about 2 lbs.)
½ cup sour cream
¼ cup mayonnaise or salad dressing
½ medium cucumber, peeled and finely chopped
½ teaspoon salt
1 teaspoon dried parsley flakes
1 teaspoon lemon juice

1. Arrange salmon steaks in 12x8-inch glass baking dish with narrow ends of steaks toward center of dish. Cover with plastic wrap.
2. MICROWAVE 6 to 7 minutes or until fish flakes apart easily. Let stand 5 minutes. Drain juices.
3. Combine remaining ingredients; spoon over salmon.
4. MICROWAVE, uncovered, 1 to 2 minutes or until sauce is heated through.   4 Servings

TIP • If using salmon fillets, use about 1½ lbs. for this cooking time.

This recipe shows how browning can be achieved by finishing the cooking under the broiler. Our home tester thought the fish flavor superb.

CRUMB-COATED FISH FILLETS

¼ cup butter or margarine
1 egg, beaten
1 tablespoon lemon juice
¾ teaspoon salt
⅛ teaspoon pepper
½ cup dry bread crumbs
2 tablespoons finely chopped almonds, if desired
1½ lbs. fish fillets, cut into serving pieces

1. MICROWAVE butter in 12x8 or 13x9-inch glass baking dish 1 to 1½ minutes or until melted.

2. Mix together egg, lemon juice, salt and pepper in shallow dish. Combine bread crumbs and almonds on waxed paper.

3. Dip fish fillets into egg mixture; coat with crumbs. Arrange in baking dish, turning to coat with butter. Drizzle any remaining egg mixture over fish; sprinkle with any remaining crumbs.

4. MICROWAVE, uncovered, 5 to 6 minutes or until steaming hot. Preheat broiler a few minutes.

5. BROIL 2 to 3 minutes or until lightly browned and fish flakes apart easily.   5 to 6 Servings

These fish fillets steam in a lemon-butter sauce.

LEMON-BUTTERED TORSK

1½ lbs. torsk (cod) fillets
2 tablespoons butter or margarine
2 tablespoons lemon juice
½ teaspoon salt
Dash pepper
Paprika

1. Arrange fillets in 10x6 or 12x8-inch glass baking dish. Dot with butter; sprinkle with remaining ingredients. Cover with plastic wrap.

2. MICROWAVE 6 to 7 minutes or until fish flakes apart easily. 5 to 6 Servings

A savory stuffing is sandwiched between fillets. Assemble ahead and then microwave just before serving.

COMPANY FILLETS AND STUFFING

¼ cup butter or margarine
1 cup chopped celery
1 small onion, chopped
1 teaspoon dried parsley flakes
2 teaspoons lemon juice
3 slices bread, cubed
2 lbs. sole or other fish fillets, cut into serving pieces
1 can (10¾ oz.) condensed cream of mushroom soup
1 tablespoon chopped pimiento
2 tablespoons sliced ripe olives
2 tablespoons dry sherry or white wine

1. MICROWAVE butter, celery and onion in uncovered glass mixing bowl 4 to 5 minutes or until vegetables are partially cooked. Stir in parsley, lemon juice and bread.

2. Arrange half of fillets in 12x8-inch glass baking dish. Spoon stuffing mixture onto each fillet. Top with remaining fillets. Cover with waxed paper.

3. MICROWAVE 8 to 9 minutes or until fish flakes apart easily. Let stand covered.

4. MICROWAVE remaining ingredients in uncovered 2-cup glass measure 3 to 4 minutes or until heated through. Spoon over fillets.   6 to 8 Servings

The almonds are toasted in butter before the fish is added since the moisture from the fish prevents browning. Pictured on page 12.

FILLETS ALMONDINE

⅓ **cup sliced or slivered almonds**
¼ **cup butter or margarine**
1½ **lbs. fish fillets, cut into serving pieces**
½ **teaspoon salt**
2 **teaspoons lemon juice**

1. MICROWAVE almonds and butter in uncovered 8-inch square glass baking dish 5 to 7 minutes or until almonds are golden brown, stirring once. Remove almonds with slotted spoon; set aside.

2. Add fish fillets to butter, turning to coat with butter. Cover with plastic wrap.

3. MICROWAVE 6 to 7 minutes or until fish flakes apart easily. Sprinkle with salt, lemon juice and almonds. If desired, garnish with lemon slices.

5 to 6 Servings

Newburg traditionally uses cooked seafood, but it is also tasty with leftover cooked fish.

EASY SEAFOOD NEWBURG

1 **can (10¾ oz.) condensed cream of shrimp soup**
1 **can (4 oz.) mushroom pieces, drained**
1 **to 2 cups diced cooked fish or seafood**
¼ **cup dry white wine or milk**
1 **teaspoon dried parsley flakes**
1 **teaspoon lemon juice**

1. Combine all ingredients in 1-quart glass casserole.

2. MICROWAVE, covered, 5 to 6 minutes or until bubbly and heated through, stirring once. Serve over toast, English muffin halves, rice or patty shells. 4 to 5 Servings

Steamed trout with a delicious spinach stuffing.

STUFFED TROUT

1 **package (10 oz.) frozen chopped spinach**
2 **tablespoons butter or margarine**
1 **small onion, chopped**
½ **teaspoon salt**
Dash pepper
¼ **cup mayonnaise or salad dressing**
4 **trout (about 8 ozs. each)**

1. MICROWAVE spinach in package 4 to 5 minutes or until thawed. Drain well and set aside.

2. MICROWAVE butter and onion in uncovered glass mixing bowl 3 to 4 minutes or until partially cooked. Stir in salt, pepper, mayonnaise and spinach. Stuff trout, using about ¼ cup stuffing for each. Arrange in 12x8 or 13x9-inch glass baking dish. Cover with waxed paper.

3. MICROWAVE 9 to 11 minutes or until fish flakes apart easily. Let stand several minutes before serving.

4 Servings

Fish sticks make a quick casserole when combined with soup and a vegetable.

FISH STICK BAKE

2 **cans (16 ozs. each) French-cut green beans, drained**
1 **package (16 oz.) breaded fish sticks**
1 **can (10¾ oz.) condensed cream of mushroom soup**
1 **teaspoon dried parsley flakes**
2 **tablespoons dry sherry or milk**

1. Place beans in 12x8-inch glass baking dish; spread evenly. Arrange fish sticks over beans; spoon soup over beans. Sprinkle with parsley and sherry. Cover with waxed paper.

2. MICROWAVE 12 to 14 minutes or until bubbly and heated through.

5 to 6 Servings

These patties are both economical and delicious.

TUNA PATTIES WITH MUSHROOM SAUCE

    2 cans (6½ ozs. each) tuna fish,
      drained
    1 can (10¾ oz.) condensed
      cream of mushroom soup
    1 egg
    2 tablespoons chopped onion
    ¼ cup dry bread crumbs
    2 tablespoons mayonnaise or
      salad dressing
    2 tablespoons milk
    1 teaspoon dried parsley flakes

1. Combine tuna, half of soup, the egg, onion and bread crumbs. Spoon into 12x8-inch glass baking dish, forming 6 mounds. Flatten to ½ inch thickness; smooth edges to form patties. Cover with waxed paper.

2. MICROWAVE 8 to 9 minutes or until set in center. Let stand covered.

3. Combine remaining soup with mayonnaise, milk and parsley in 2-cup glass measure.

4. MICROWAVE 1½ to 2½ minutes or until heated through. Serve sauce over patties.   6 Servings

This recipe was a favorite when prepared in class. Since all the ingredients except the egg are cooked, it just needs to heat through.

TUNA-NOODLE CASSEROLE

    8 ozs. noodles (about 4 cups)
    1 can (6½ oz.) tuna fish, drained
    1 can (10¾ oz.) condensed
      cream of mushroom soup
    1 cup cubed Cheddar or
      American cheese
    ¾ cup milk
    1 egg, beaten
    ¼ cup crushed soda crackers

1. Cook noodles as directed on package; drain.

2. Combine noodles, tuna, soup and cheese in 1½-quart glass casserole. Combine milk and egg; pour over noodle mixture. Sprinkle with crumbs.

3. MICROWAVE, uncovered, 9 to 11 minutes or until casserole is hot in center (155°).   5 to 6 Servings

Dill pickle adds an interesting touch to this salmon loaf. Notice the difference in cooking time when the shape changes from a loaf to individual patties (see Tip). Delicious served with a cheese, egg or mushroom sauce.

SALMON LOAF

    2 cans (7½ oz. each) salmon,
      drained
    2 eggs
    2 slices bread, cubed
    ½ cup milk
    ¼ cup chopped dill pickle
    2 tablespoons finely chopped
      onion
    1 tablespoon lemon juice
    1 teaspoon dried parsley flakes
    ¼ teaspoon salt
    ⅛ teaspoon pepper

1. Combine salmon and eggs in mixing bowl; mix with fork to combine. Stir in remaining ingredients, mixing well. Spoon into 8x4-inch glass loaf dish. Cover with waxed paper.

2. MICROWAVE 8 to 10 minutes or until center is hot and begins to set (155°), rotating dish once or twice. Let stand several minutes before serving. If desired, garnish with lemon and dill pickle slices.   5 to 6 Servings

TIP ● SALMON PATTIES: Shape mixture into 6 patties. Arrange in 12x8-inch glass baking dish; cover with waxed paper. Microwave 7 to 8 minutes or until set.

Lobster tails are quick and easy prepared in the microwave oven. See page 10 for defrosting directions.

LOBSTER TAILS

1. Split each 8-oz. thawed lobster tail through top shell. Release lobster from shell, leaving meat connected to shell at top end. Place meat on top of shell.
2. Arrange tails in shallow glass casserole. Brush with melted butter; sprinkle with paprika.
3. MICROWAVE, covered, until meat is firm and translucent:
   2 tails - 5 to 6 minutes
   4 tails - 10 to 11 minutes
Let stand a few minutes before serving.

These vegetables require partial cooking before the other ingredients are added.

SWEET-SOUR SHRIMP

1 small onion, sliced
2 stalks celery, sliced
2 tablespoons butter or margarine
¼ cup sugar
3 tablespoons cornstarch
¼ teaspoon ground ginger
1 teaspoon paprika
1 can (13¼ oz.) pineapple tidbits, undrained
2 tablespoons soy sauce
¼ cup vinegar
12 ozs. frozen uncooked shrimp
1 green pepper, cut into strips

1. Combine onion, celery and butter in 2-quart glass casserole.
2. MICROWAVE, covered, 4 to 5 minutes or until vegetables are partially cooked. Stir in remaining ingredients.
3. MICROWAVE, covered, 14 to 16 minutes or until mixture is bubbly and shrimp are firm and pink. If desired, serve over rice.   5 to 6 Servings

The shrimp in this recipe thaw and cook while the remaining ingredients are heating. Pictured on page 12.

ORIENTAL SHRIMP AND VEGETABLES

2 tablespoons butter or margarine
4 green onions, sliced
1 can (6 oz.) water chestnuts, drained and sliced
1 can (6 oz.) bamboo shoots, drained
1 can (4 oz.) mushroom pieces, drained
1 teaspoon instant chicken bouillon
⅛ teaspoon ginger
1 tablespoon cornstarch
3 tablespoons soy sauce
⅓ cup water
12 ozs. frozen uncooked shrimp

1. Combine butter and onions in 2-quart glass casserole.
2. MICROWAVE, uncovered, 2 to 3 minutes or until bubbly. Stir in remaining ingredients.
3. MICROWAVE, covered, 11 to 13 minutes or until mixture boils and shrimp are firm, stirring once or twice. If desired, serve over rice.
                    5 to 6 Servings

TIP • The frozen uncooked shrimp contain more water than either thawed or frozen cooked shrimp. When you are substituting one of these, add ¼ to ½ cup additional water to form a sauce-like consistency.

Poultry

ABOUT POULTRY: Poultry cooks nicely in the microwave oven, and usually is in the oven long enough for some browning to develop. Ingredients like paprika and soy sauce also help to enhance this browning.

Waxed paper is often used as a covering for poultry. It helps to hold in the heat, yet allows the poultry to brown and the skin to crisp.

Most of these recipes using fryers are cooked with a full power or high setting. With whole birds like capon and turkey, best results are obtained by reducing the power to a lower setting during the last part of the cooking time. Since the bird finishes cooking more slowly, a shorter standing time before carving can be used.

This crumb coating stays crisper when not covered. If spattering is a problem, cover lightly with paper towels.

OVEN-BAKED CHICKEN

  1 package (2⅜ oz.) seasoned
    coating mix for chicken
2½ to 3-lb. frying chicken, cut up

1. Place coating mix in bag provided with mix. Add moist chicken pieces and shake to coat with crumbs. Arrange skin-side-up in 12x8-inch glass baking dish.
2. MICROWAVE, uncovered, 25 to 30 minutes or until chicken is done.
                              4 to 6 Servings

Pictured: Stuffed Cornish Hens, page 22.

FRYING CHICKEN REMINDERS
• Wash chicken with cold water before using. The moisture also helps any coating cling to the surface.
• Cut chicken into as uniformly-sized pieces as possible. Then arrange in the baking dish with the larger or thicker pieces toward the corners and the thinner, smaller pieces toward the center. If cooking the gizzard, heart and liver too, place these toward the center tucked under other pieces of chicken. This prevents concentrated cooking that makes them give a loud popping noise.
• The chicken pieces will brown as they cook. If additional browning or crisping is desired, just place the chicken under the broiler or browning element for a few minutes.

Cornflakes make the golden coating for this chicken.

GOLDEN BAKED CHICKEN

  ⅓ cup butter or margarine
  1 clove garlic, minced
  1 cup cornflake crumbs
  ¼ cup finely chopped almonds
    or other nuts
  1 tablespoon dried parsley flakes
  1 teaspoon salt
  ¼ teaspoon poultry seasoning
  ⅛ teaspoon pepper
2½ to 3-lb. frying chicken, cut up

1. MICROWAVE butter and garlic in 12x8-inch glass baking dish about 1 minute or until melted.
2. Combine crumbs, almonds, parsley, salt, poultry seasoning and pepper on waxed paper. Dip chicken pieces into melted butter; roll in crumb mixture. Arrange skin-side-up in baking dish. Sprinkle any remaining crumbs over chicken.
3. MICROWAVE, uncovered, 25 to 30 minutes or until chicken is done.
                              4 to 6 Servings

The flavors in this recipe are superb. It may become a favorite.

CREAMY BAKED CHICKEN

¼ **cup dry bread crumbs**
2 **tablespoons grated Parmesan cheese**
1 **tablespoon dried parsley flakes**
½ **teaspoon garlic salt**
⅛ **teaspoon pepper**
2½ **to 3-lb. frying chicken, cut up**
1 **can (10¾ oz.) condensed cream of mushroom soup**
2 **tablespoons milk**
Grated Parmesan cheese
Paprika

1. Combine bread crumbs, cheese, parsley, garlic salt and pepper. Coat chicken with mixture; arrange skin-side-up in 12x8-inch glass baking dish. Cover with waxed paper.

2. MICROWAVE 20 to 22 minutes or until chicken is just about done. Combine soup and milk; spoon over chicken. Sprinkle with cheese and paprika.

3. MICROWAVE, covered with waxed paper, 5 to 6 minutes or until chicken is done.   4 to 6 Servings

CHICKEN AND STUFFING

1 **package (6 oz.) saucepan stuffing mix**
1½ **to 1¾ cups water**
1 **can (4 oz.) mushroom pieces, drained**
2½ **to 3-lb. frying chicken, cut up**
¼ **cup butter or margarine**
Salt and pepper
Paprika

1. Combine stuffing mix (with seasonings), water and mushrooms in 12x8-inch glass baking dish. Arrange chicken pieces skin-side-up over stuffing.

2. MICROWAVE butter in small glass dish ½ to 1 minute or until melted. Brush or drizzle over chicken. Season chicken with salt and pepper; sprinkle with paprika. Cover with waxed paper.

3. MICROWAVE 30 to 35 minutes or until chicken is done.   5 to 6 Servings

Frying chicken cooks atop a creamy rice mixture. With the additional ingredients, the time increases slightly.

OVEN CHICKEN AND RICE

1½ **cups uncooked long-grain rice**
1 **can (4 oz.) mushroom pieces, drained**
1 **stalk celery, chopped**
2 **tablespoons chopped onion**
1 **can (10¾ oz.) condensed cream of chicken soup**
2 **cups water**
2½ **to 3-lb. frying chicken, cut up**
1 **teaspoon salt**
2 **tablespoons butter or margarine**
Paprika

1. Combine rice, mushrooms, celery, onion, soup and water in 12x8-inch glass baking dish; mix well. Arrange chicken pieces skin-side-up over rice; sprinkle with salt.

2. MICROWAVE butter in small glass dish about ½ minute or until melted. Drizzle or brush butter over chicken; sprinkle with paprika. Cover with waxed paper.

3. MICROWAVE 30 to 35 minutes or until chicken and rice are done.
                              5 to 6 Servings

Use your microwave oven to quickly steam chicken before broiling or barbecuing. The broiling or barbecuing is much faster and the finished chicken is more moist.

BROILED OR BARBECUED CHICKEN

1. Arrange a 2½ to 3-lb. cut-up frying chicken in 12x8-inch glass baking dish. Cover with waxed paper.

2. MICROWAVE 15 minutes.

3. Place chicken pieces on broiler rack or grill; brush with favorite sauce.

4. BROIL or BARBECUE 10 to 15 minutes or until golden brown, turning once.   4 to 6 Servings

CASSEROLE REMINDERS

• Since the chicken or turkey is already cooked, the other ingredients in the casserole determine the cooking time. Some casseroles only need heating, while others need to cook certain ingredients.

• Covering speeds the heating or cooking of most casseroles. Stirring also helps when it is possible. Coverings are omitted, though, when there is a cheese or other topping that may melt onto the covering.

Our home tester thought this one of the best recipes she had tried for leftover poultry.

CHICKEN AND RICE CASSEROLE

    1 cup uncooked long-grain rice
    1 can (16 oz.) cut green beans, undrained
    1 can (10¾ oz.) condensed cream of mushroom soup
    1 small onion, chopped
  ½ cup mayonnaise or salad dressing
  ¾ cup water
  2 to 3 cups cubed cooked chicken or turkey
    2 tablespoons chopped pimiento
    2 teaspoons instant chicken bouillon

1. Combine all ingredients in 2-quart glass casserole.

2. MICROWAVE, covered, 30 to 35 minutes or until rice is tender, stirring 2 or 3 times.   **4 to 6 Servings**

Chicken, ham and Swiss cheese — sure to be a favorite.

CHICKEN AND HAM ROLL-UPS

 1½ cups finely chopped cooked chicken or turkey
    1 green onion, sliced
    1 can (10¾ oz.) condensed cream of chicken soup
    5 to 6 slices boiled ham (sandwich type)
  ¼ cup milk
  ½ cup shredded Swiss cheese
    Paprika

1. Combine chicken, onion and ⅓ cup of soup. Spoon about ¼ cup onto each ham slice. Roll up; secure edges with toothpicks. Place in 10x6-inch glass baking dish. Combine remaining soup and milk; spoon over rolls. Sprinkle with cheese and paprika.

2. MICROWAVE, uncovered, 5 to 6 minutes or until heated through. If desired, serve with cooked rice or noodles.   **5 to 6 Servings**

TIP • For a more complete casserole, place a layer of cooked rice in baking dish before adding ham rolls. Continue as directed, but increase cooking time to 8 to 9 minutes.

Turn leftovers into a company casserole with this recipe.

CHICKEN AND ARTICHOKE CASSEROLE

  ¼ cup butter or margarine
    2 cups (1 pt.) sliced fresh mushrooms
  ⅓ cup all-purpose flour
    1 cup light cream
    1 cup water
    1 teaspoon instant chicken bouillon
  ½ teaspoon salt
    1 can (14 oz.) artichoke hearts, drained and halved
    2 to 3 cups cubed cooked chicken or turkey
    2 tablespoons dry sherry, if desired
    1 tablespoon chopped pimiento
  ¼ cup grated Parmesan cheese
    Hot cooked noodles

1. MICROWAVE butter and mushrooms in uncovered 2-quart glass casserole 5 to 6 minutes or until tender, stirring once. Stir in flour, cream, water, bouillon and salt.

2. MICROWAVE, uncovered, 5 to 6 minutes or until mixture boils, stirring once. Stir in remaining ingredients except noodles.

3. MICROWAVE, covered, 8 to 10 minutes or until heated through and flavors are blended, stirring once. Serve over noodles. If desired, sprinkle with parsley and additional Parmesan cheese.   **About 6 Servings**

ROAST POULTRY REMINDERS

- Use pieces of foil to slow the cooking of areas that may otherwise overcook. This includes the wing tips, narrow part of the legs and sometimes the high point of the breast bone.
- The larger the bird, the more important turning is to achieve an evenly cooked bird. On very large turkeys, it may be desirable to turn during cooking so that each side is up as well as breast-up and breast-down.
- The inside of the thigh is usually the slowest area to cook on roast poultry. If this area is not completely thawed before starting to cook, it will be especially difficult to achieve an evenly cooked bird.
- A waxed paper covering helps to hold in the heat and prevents spattering in the microwave oven.
- There are special thermometers for microwave use. Ordinary meat thermometers are not used in the microwave oven (there are some especially designed for this use).
- A 10 to 20 minute standing time before carving helps the juices to set in the meat, keeping the meat more moist.
- The probe can be used for cooking turkeys. Other types of poultry are not large enough to assure accurate measurements. Wait to insert the probe until after the last turning of the bird.

Use this recipe or your own favorite recipe for stuffing poultry.

BREAD STUFFING

 ½ cup butter or margarine
 1 medium onion, chopped
 2 stalks celery, chopped
10 cups dry bread cubes
 1 tablespoon dried parsley flakes
 1 teaspoon salt
 2 teaspoons poultry seasoning
 ¼ teaspoon pepper
 ½ cup chicken broth or water

1. Combine butter, onion and celery in large glass mixing bowl.

2. MICROWAVE, uncovered, 5 to 6 minutes or until vegetables are partially cooked. Stir in remaining ingredients.
      Stuffing for 12 to 16-lb. Turkey

TIPS • For Roast Chicken or Capon, use half the ingredient amounts. Microwave in step 2 for 3 to 4 minutes.
      • When there is more dressing than will fit inside the bird, place in a covered casserole and microwave 5 to 10 minutes or until heated through. You may wish to increase the amount of broth.

This two-step cooking method gives beautifully cooked Cornish hens. Pictured on page 18.

STUFFED CORNISH HENS

 ⅓ cup butter or margarine
 ¼ cup sesame seed
 1 stalk celery, chopped
 1 small onion, chopped
 4 cups (4 slices) bread cubes
 ½ teaspoon salt
 ½ teaspoon poultry seasoning
 1 teaspoon Worcestershire sauce
 4 Cornish hens (about 1 lb. each)
 3 tablespoons butter or margarine, melted
 1 teaspoon paprika

1. Combine butter, sesame seed, celery and onion in glass mixing bowl.

2. MICROWAVE, uncovered, 4 to 5 minutes or until lightly toasted, stirring once or twice. Stir in remaining ingredients, except Cornish hens and butter.

3. Stuff Cornish hens with bread mixture; secure openings with toothpicks or wooden skewers. Place breast-side-down in 12x8 or 13x9-inch glass baking dish. Combine butter and paprika. Brush hens with butter; cover with waxed paper.

4. MICROWAVE 20 minutes; turn breast-side-up and brush with remaining butter. Cover.

5. MICROWAVE 20 to 22 minutes or until tender and legs can be moved easily.   4 Servings

TIP • Hens can also be finished in a 400° oven for about 15 minutes or until skin is crisp.

PREPARING WHOLE BIRDS FOR ROASTING

1. Wash bird and set aside giblets to use as desired. Sprinkle cavity with salt. Stuff neck and main cavity with favorite stuffing or leave unstuffed. Secure openings with toothpicks or wooden skewers. Tie legs together and wings to body with string. Wrap tips of legs and wings with small pieces of foil to prevent overcooking.

2. Place bird breast-side-down in 12x8 or 13x9-inch glass baking dish, using rack if desired. Brush with butter mixture.

3. MICROWAVE as directed below.

ROAST CHICKEN

1. Prepare a 3 to 5-lb. chicken for roasting as directed above. Use 1 tablespoon melted butter and ½ teaspoon paprika to brush bird.

2. MICROWAVE, covered with waxed paper, 25 to 40 minutes (about 8 minutes per lb.), turning breast-side-up about halfway through cooking time. Thermometer should register 185°. Let stand a few minutes before carving.

6 to 8 Servings

ROAST DUCKLING

1. Prepare a 4 to 6-lb. duckling for roasting as directed above. Omit butter mixture.

2. MICROWAVE, covered with waxed paper, 25 to 35 minutes (6 minutes per lb.), turning breast-side-up and draining fat about halfway through cooking time. Remove foil pieces. Brush skin with ¼ cup orange marmalade.

3. BAKE, uncovered, at 400° for 30 to 45 minutes or until skin is crispy brown and legs can be moved easily.

4 Servings

TIP • For extra crisp skin, turn duck over once during baking in step 3, brushing with orange marmalade.

ROAST CAPON

1. Prepare a 5 to 8-lb. capon for roasting as directed. Use 2 tablespoons melted butter and ½ teaspoon paprika to brush bird.

2. MICROWAVE, covered with waxed paper, 40 to 60 minutes (about 8 minutes per lb.), turning breast-side-up about halfway through cooking time. Thermometer should register 185°. Let stand 10 minutes before carving.

10 to 14 Servings

ROAST TURKEY

1. Prepare a 10 to 14-lb. turkey for roasting as directed above except place breast-side-up. Brush with half of a mixture of ¼ cup melted butter and 1 teaspoon paprika. Cover with waxed paper.

2. MICROWAVE 30 minutes. Turn breast-side-down. Cover with waxed paper.

3. MICROWAVE 30 minutes.

4. MICROWAVE medium-high (70%) 20 minutes. Turn breast-side-up. Brush with remaining butter mixture. Cover with waxed paper. Insert probe or microwave meat thermometer if desired.

5. MICROWAVE medium-high (70%) 20 to 40 minutes or until meat is no longer pink and meat thermometer registers 165°. Let stand 15 minutes before carving.

TIP • If high point of breast becomes overly browned, cover area with about 2-inch piece of foil.

Meats

ABOUT MEATS: Many meats cook very successfully in the microwave oven and this chapter includes a sampling. Since the size and shape of the meat is a major factor in the cooking technique and time, the chapter is organized according to cut of meat. Included with each section are reminders about cooking the particular cuts.

Most meats develop some browning when cooked for more than 10 minutes, and cured meats like bacon, ham and sausage will brown in less time than this. When a meat cooks in less than 10 minutes, gravy mix or a special sprinkle-on browning seasoning can be sprinkled or brushed on the meat before cooking. Most of these include color and flavor ingredients similar to those achieved when meat is browned in a frying pan.

When cooking meats in the microwave oven, keep in mind that tender meats like pork, lamb, veal and tender cuts of beef cook very well and quickly with microwaves. Less tender cuts of beef need long, slow simmering to become tender. This can be achieved in the microwave oven and there are some recipes included for these meats. However, there is very little time advantage.

ROAST REMINDERS
• Regular meat thermometers should not be used in the microwave oven.
• Either boneless or bone-in roasts can be used for the times given.
• Allow ¼ to ⅓ lb. of boneless roast per serving and about ½ lb. per serving when the roast contains a bone.
• Pot roasts require long, slow simmering to become tender. If you wish to use the microwave oven, follow the technique for the Beef Stew recipe, page 32.

BEEF, LAMB OR PORK ROAST

1. Place a 3 to 5-lb. roast fat-side-down in shallow glass baking dish (use a microwave roasting rack in dish if desired). Season meat with salt, pepper and other desired seasoning. Cover with waxed paper.

2. MICROWAVE according to timetable below, turning meat fat-side-up about halfway through cooking time. If desired, insert probe or microwave meat thermometer after turning fat-side-up.

3. After reaching doneness specified in guide, let stand (covered) 10 to 20 minutes before carving.

Timetable

Type Roast	Microwave Time	Variable Power	Doneness or Probe Guide
Beef (rare)	8 to 9 minutes/lb.	medium-high (70%)	125°
Beef (medium)	9 to 10 minutes/lb.	medium-high (70%)	140°
Beef (well)	11 to 12 minutes/lb.	medium-high (70%)	160°
Pork	10 to 11 minutes/lb.	medium-high (70%)	160°
Lamb	9 to 10 minutes/lb.	medium-high (70%)	160°

TIPS • For smaller roasts, increase microwave time ½ to 1 minute per lb. For larger roasts, decrease microwave time ½ to 1 minute per lb.
• For a glazed pork or lamb roast, brush apple, currant or mint jelly over roast during last 5 to 7 minutes cooking time.

Pictured, top to bottom: Lamb Stew, page 32, Pork Chop and Stuffing Bake, page 30, and Beef Roast, this page.

COOKED MEAT REMINDERS

• Leftover cooked meat reheats very well if heated just to the serving temperature. If overheated, the meat may become tough and dry. For ease in heating, keep the slices thin and arrange on a plate so the meat is of about even thickness. A light covering of waxed paper helps hold in the heat.

• When cooked meat is used in a casserole, there is less chance of overcooking because of the additional ingredients present. Usually the cooking time for these dishes depends upon the additional ingredients — some will need only to be heated while others will require some cooking.

• Don't expect the meats to become more tender during the heating unless you allow them to simmer by using a low setting or on-off cooking.

• Most hams and ham slices are cooked when purchased, so these recipes use the same type of cooking techniques as leftover cooked meats.

A quick stew that starts with leftover roast.

DAY-AFTER STEW

 2 to 3 cups cubed pork, beef or lamb
 1½ cups gravy
 ¼ to ½ cup water
 1 medium onion, quartered
 3 medium potatoes, peeled and cubed
 4 medium carrots, sliced
 1 teaspoon salt
 1 teaspoon Worcestershire sauce
 ⅛ teaspoon pepper

1. Combine all ingredients in 2 or 2½-quart glass casserole.

2. MICROWAVE, covered, 25 to 30 minutes or until vegetables are tender, stirring 2 or 3 times.   5 to 6 Servings

TIP • If you do not have leftover gravy, use 1 can condensed cream of mushroom or celery soup and increase water to ¾ cup.

If you watch your timing carefully, you can keep leftovers from a rare roast, rare or medium rare.

REHEATING SLICED COOKED ROAST

1. Arrange ¼-inch thick slices of roast on glass serving plate. Cover with waxed paper.

2. MICROWAVE until steaming hot:
  2 slices -   1 to 1½ minutes
  4 slices - 1½ to   2 minutes
  8 slices -   3 to   4 minutes
 12 slices -   5 to   6 minutes
Allow to stand a few minutes before serving.

This spicy sauce is good with any cooked meat.

BARBECUED MEAT SLICES

 1 medium onion, sliced
 2 tablespoons butter or margarine
 1 cup catsup
 2 tablespoons brown sugar
 2 tablespoons lemon juice
 1 tablespoon Worcestershire sauce
 1 teaspoon prepared mustard
 ½ teaspoon salt
 ¼ teaspoon pepper
 8 to 10 thin slices cooked beef or pork

1. Combine onion and butter in 1½-quart glass casserole.

2. MICROWAVE, uncovered, 3 to 4 minutes or until onion is tender. Stir in remaining ingredients except meat; mix well. Add meat, coating each slice with sauce.

3. MICROWAVE, covered, 10 to 15 minutes or until heated through, rearranging once or twice. Serve over rice or toast.   5 to 6 Servings

TIP • Meat for this recipe should already be tender. If not, allow to simmer using technique in Swiss Steak recipe, page 31.

Your family will never identify this as "leftovers".

PORK AND RICE BAKE

**3 cups cooked rice
1 can (16 oz.) green beans or
other favorite vegetable,
drained
5 to 6 slices cooked pork roast
Mornay Sauce, page 65
Grated Parmesan cheese**

1. Layer rice, vegetable and meat in 1½ or 2-quart glass casserole. Prepare Mornay Sauce as directed; pour over meat slices. Sprinkle with Parmesan cheese.
2. MICROWAVE, covered, 8 to 10 minutes or until heated through.

5 to 6 Servings

TIP • If desired, prepare Fluffy White Rice, page 59, through step 2. Then top with vegetable, meat, sauce and cheese. Reduce microwave time to 5 to 6 minutes.

A good casserole for using the last of the ham.

HAM AND ASPARAGUS CASSEROLE

**8 ozs. noodles (about 4 cups)
2 to 3 cups cubed cooked ham
1 can (10¾ oz.) condensed
cream of mushroom soup
1 can (16 oz.) cut asparagus,
undrained
4 ozs. sliced Swiss cheese
Paprika**

1. Cook noodles as directed on package; drain. Combine noodles, ham, soup and asparagus in 2-quart glass casserole. Stir lightly to combine. Top with cheese slices; sprinkle with paprika.
2. MICROWAVE, covered, 8 to 10 minutes or until hot and bubbly (155°).

5 to 6 Servings

TIPS • Canned cut green beans or whole kernel corn, undrained, can be substituted for asparagus.

• *Variable Power:* Microwave medium-high (70%) 12 to 14 minutes.

Most hams are precooked so they need only be heated, and this heating can be done with just microwave cooking. If you have an uncooked ham, cook it like a pork roast.

GLAZED BAKED HAM

**3-lb. ready-to-eat ham
Whole cloves
3 tablespoons brown sugar
1 tablespoon orange or apple
juice**

1. Place ham fat-side-down in 8-inch round glass baking dish. Cover with waxed paper.
2. MICROWAVE 12 minutes.
3. Turn ham fat-side-up. Slash through fat at 1-inch intervals; insert cloves into squares. Combine brown sugar and juice; spoon or brush over ham.
4. MICROWAVE, uncovered, 6 to 7 minutes or until heated through (120°).

8 to 12 Servings

TIPS • For other sized hams, allow 6 minutes per lb. heating time. Turn ham over about ⅔ through cooking time. Add glaze during last 5 to 7 minutes cooking time.

• *Variable Power:* In step 2, microwave medium-high (70%) 20 minutes. Microwave medium (50%) 8 to 12 minutes in step 4.

Buy a large ham and remove a few slices to use for this recipe.

SLICED HAM WITH ORANGE SAUCE

**6 slices cooked ham, cut
¼-inch thick
6 whole cloves
¼ cup packed brown sugar
1 tablespoon cornstarch
Dash ginger
½ cup orange juice
1 orange, sliced**

1. Insert a whole clove into each ham slice. Arrange slices in shallow 1½-quart glass casserole. Combine brown sugar, cornstarch, ginger and orange juice; spoon over ham.
2. MICROWAVE, covered, 9 to 11 minutes or until hot and bubbly. Garnish with orange slices.

5 to 6 Servings

WIENER, SAUSAGE AND BACON REMINDERS

• Wieners are prepared from cooked ingredients so only need to be heated. Occasionally the fat content may vary within the wiener and so one part will heat faster than the remainder. A standing time is necessary to even out this heating.

• Bacon is always a favorite for cooking in the microwave oven. It browns and becomes crisp without any turning or watching. Because of the various curing processes used with different brands, there may be more of a variance in cooking times than with most other meats.

• Sausage (except brown and serve types) is uncooked so needs to cook longer than wieners. Usually some browning will develop during this time. For additional browning, a browning element or grill can be used.

Use these times as a guide, but remember bacon cooking time varies with brand and thickness.

BACON

1. Arrange bacon slices in layer on paper towel in shallow glass baking dish. Layer toweling between each additional layer of bacon and cover top with layer of paper towel.

2. MICROWAVE until bacon is browned and crisp:

    2 slices - 1½ to 2½ minutes
    4 slices -   3 to   4 minutes
    6 slices - 3½ to 4½ minutes
    10 slices - 5½ to 6½ minutes

Sausages will develop a small amount of browning. For additional browning, use a browning skillet.

LINK SAUSAGES

1. Arrange 8 ozs. link sausages in 9-inch round glass pie plate. Cover with paper towel.

2. MICROWAVE 4 to 5 minutes or until sausages are done. Drain on paper towel before serving.

                       3 to 4 Servings

TIP • *Browning Element:* Use upper position and microwave 2 minutes. Then brown 6 to 8 minutes, turning links once.

Wieners heat very quickly.

WIENERS

1. Place wieners in covered glass casserole.

2. MICROWAVE until steaming hot:
    2 wieners - ½ to   1 minute
    4 wieners - 1½ to   2 minutes
    6 wieners - 2½ to   3 minutes
    10 wieners -   4 to 4½ minutes
Allow to stand a few minutes before serving.

Wieners require a little longer heating time when combined with other ingredients.

POTATO-WIENER BAKE

  1½ cups water
   ¾ teaspoon salt
   3 tablespoons butter or margarine
   ¾ cup milk
   2 cups mashed potato flakes
   ½ cup cottage cheese
   6 to 8 wieners
   1 cup shredded Cheddar or American cheese
   Poppy seed, if desired

1. Combine water, salt and butter in 1-quart glass casserole.

2. MICROWAVE, covered, 3 to 4 minutes or until mixture boils. Stir in milk and potato flakes; let stand a few minutes. Stir in cottage cheese. Spread in 10x6-inch glass baking dish. Split wieners almost through lengthwise; place split-side up on potato mixture, pressing into mixture. Sprinkle with cheese and poppy seed. Cover with waxed paper.

3. MICROWAVE 4 to 5 minutes or until heated through (150°), rotating dish once.   6 to 8 Servings

TIP • When substituting granular-type mashed potatoes, increase amount to 2½ cups.

Pictured: Chinese Beef and Vegetables, page 31.

CHOP AND RIB REMINDERS

• Use your microwave oven for cooking chops in a sauce. For pan-fried chops, either prebrown the chops or use a browning grill or skillet.

• Allow about 25 to 30 minutes to cook 5 to 6 chops until tender. They will be done before this time, but the additional time improves the flavor and tenderness. This cooking can be done with a full power or medium-high setting.

• Lamb, pork and veal chops, whether shoulder or loin, can be cooked using the methods given on this page.

• Pork ribs are cooked similarly to chops, but because they contain additional fat, they require a precooking step before the sauce ingredients are added.

Pork chops simmer in a flavorful sweet and sour sauce. If you wish, allow the chops to stand during the last part of the cooking time while you cook a vegetable.

SWEET-SOUR PORK CHOPS

   3 tablespoons all-purpose flour
½ cup packed brown sugar
¼ teaspoon salt
   5 to 6 pork chops, cut ½-inch thick
¼ cup soy sauce
⅓ cup vinegar
¾ cup water
   1 small onion, chopped
   1 small green pepper, sliced

1. Combine flour, brown sugar and salt; coat chops with mixture. Arrange chops in 12x8-inch glass baking dish; sprinkle remaining flour mixture over chops.

2. Combine soy sauce, vinegar and water; pour over chops. Top with onion and green pepper.

3. MICROWAVE, covered with waxed paper, 25 to 30 minutes or until chops are tender.　　　5 to 6 Servings

TIP • *Variable Power:* Microwave medium-high (70%) 40 to 45 minutes.

These chops develop a nice brown color and flavor. Pictured on page 24.

PORK CHOP AND STUFFING BAKE

   4 cups dry bread cubes
   1 small onion, chopped
½ cup chopped celery
¼ teaspoon salt
¼ teaspoon poultry seasoning
½ cup water
   5 to 6 pork chops, cut ½-inch thick
   1 can (10¾ oz.) condensed cream of chicken soup

1. Combine bread cubes, onion, celery, salt, poultry seasoning and water in 12x8-inch glass baking dish; mix to combine. Arrange chops over stuffing; spoon soup over chops. Cover with waxed paper.

2. MICROWAVE 25 to 30 minutes or until chops are tender, rotating dish once.　　　5 to 6 Servings

TIP • *Variable Power:* Microwave medium-high (70%) 40 to 45 minutes.

This was another favorite of a home tester — it is quick and simple as well as flavorful.

BARBECUED RIBS

   3 to 4 lbs. country-style ribs or spareribs
½ cup catsup
   1 clove garlic, minced
   2 tablespoons brown sugar
   1 tablespoon Worcestershire sauce
   1 tablespoon lemon juice
½ teaspoon salt
½ teaspoon dry mustard
½ teaspoon prepared horseradish

1. Cut meat into single-rib pieces. Arrange in 12x8-inch glass baking dish. Cover with waxed paper.

2. MICROWAVE 12 to 15 minutes or until meat is no longer pink, rearranging once. Drain fat.

3. Combine remaining ingredients; brush over ribs, using all of sauce.

4. MICROWAVE, covered, 8 to 10 minutes or until ribs are done. If desired, garnish with lemon slices.
　　　6 to 8 Servings

STEAK REMINDERS

• Tender steaks such as rib or sirloin can be cooked quickly in a sauce or browned on the browning grill using the microwave oven.

• The microwave oven also reheats or finishes cooking tender steaks that were cooked on the grill or under the broiler. Just watch the time carefully as usually less than a minute per steak is ample to reheat or finish cooking.

• Less tender steaks, like round or chuck, require long, slow simmering to become tender. This can be accomplished in the microwave oven by using a simmer setting (30% power) or an on-off cooking technique. The addition of an acid food like tomatoes or wine also helps tenderize these cuts of meat.

Because you start with a less tender meat, it is necessary to allow about 1¼ hours cooking time. If you have a simmer setting on your oven, you can just set the timer for one hour and eliminate the standing times.

SWISS STEAK

   1½ to 2 lbs. round steak, cut
      ½-inch thick
   ¼ cup all-purpose flour
   1¼ teaspoons salt
   ¼ teaspoon pepper
    2 tablespoons cooking oil
    1 medium onion, sliced
    1 can (16 oz.) stewed tomatoes,
      undrained

1. Cut steak into serving pieces; pound with meat mallet to help tenderize. Coat pieces with mixture of flour, salt and pepper.

2. Heat oil in freezer-to-range glass ceramic skillet over medium-high heat. Add meat and onion and brown on both sides. Add tomatoes and any remaining flour mixture.

3. MICROWAVE, covered, 5 minutes or until mixture boils. Let stand 15 minutes. Repeat this step 3 to 4 times or until meat is desired tenderness.

                              6 to 8 Servings

TIPS • *Variable Power:* Microwave high 5 minutes. Then, microwave low (30%) 1 to 1¼ hours or until tender, rearranging meat once.

   • Swiss steak is easily prepared in a cooking/roasting bag. Just pierce bag so steam can escape.

This makes an attractive company dish. Since you start with a tender cut of meat, the cooking goes very quickly. Pictured on page 29.

CHINESE BEEF AND VEGETABLES

   1 small head cauliflower
   1 lb. beef tenderloin tip, sliced
      paper thin
   1 small onion, thinly sliced
   1 clove garlic, minced
   ¼ cup soy sauce
   1 package (7 oz.) frozen
      pea pods
   1 can (10½ oz.) condensed
      beef broth
   ¼ cup cornstarch
   Hot cooked rice

1. Separate cauliflower into flowerettes; cut each into ¼-inch slices. Place in 2-quart glass casserole. Add beef, onion and garlic. Pour soy sauce over mixture; stir lightly to coat evenly.

2. MICROWAVE, covered, 9 to 11 minutes, stirring once. Add frozen pea pods.

3. MICROWAVE, covered, 2 to 3 minutes or until pea pods are thawed and cauliflower is tender-crisp. Set aside.

4. Combine broth and cornstarch in 2-cup glass measure. Stir in juices from meat.

5. MICROWAVE 3½ to 4½ minutes or until mixture boils, stirring once. Stir into beef mixture. Serve over rice.

                              4 to 5 Servings

TIP • If pea pods are not available, an 8-oz. package frozen cut asparagus may be substituted.

CUBED MEAT REMINDERS

• Pork and lamb are usually quite tender so will cook and become tender within the same time other ingredients are cooked.

• Beef cubes are usually from less tender sections and require long, slow simmering. If you wish to use the microwave oven for this cooking, use either a slow simmer setting or the on-off cooking technique. Once the vegetables are added, regular microwave cooking is used to quickly cook them and finish cooking the meat.

Allow about 1¾ hours for this recipe. Since the meat must cook slowly to become tender, there is really no time saved.

BEEF STEW

  1½ **lbs. boneless beef stew meat**
    ¼ **cup all-purpose flour**
    2 teaspoons salt
    ¼ **teaspoon pepper**
    2 tablespoons cooking oil
    2 stalks celery, cut up
    2 medium onions, quartered
    1 bay leaf
    1 tablespoon vinegar
    3 cups water
    1 cup whole fresh mushrooms
    4 potatoes, peeled and cut into pieces
    6 carrots, cut into 1-inch pieces
    ½ **cup water**
    3 tablespoons all-purpose flour
    1 teaspoon salt

1. Coat meat with mixture of ¼ cup flour, 2 teaspoons salt and the pepper. Heat oil in 4-quart freezer-to-range glass ceramic Dutch oven or casserole over medium-high heat. Add meat and brown on all sides. Add celery, onions, bay leaf, vinegar and 3 cups water.

2. MICROWAVE, covered, 8 to 10 minutes or until mixture boils. Let stand 20 minutes.

3. MICROWAVE, covered, 4 to 5 minutes or until mixture boils again. Let stand 20 minutes.

4. Repeat step 3. Add mushrooms, potatoes and carrots. Combine ½ cup water, 3 tablespoons flour and 1 teaspoon salt; stir into meat mixture.

5. MICROWAVE, covered, 25 to 30 minutes or until vegetables are desired doneness. Let stand a few minutes; remove bay leaf before serving.
                    5 to 6 Servings

TIP • *Variable Power:* Microwave high 8 to 10 minutes. Then, microwave low (30%) 1¼ to 1½ hours or until meat is tender. Add remaining ingredients. Microwave medium-high (70%) for 30 to 40 minutes.

Gravy mix adds color and flavor to this quick-cooking stew. Pictured on page 24.

PORK OR LAMB STEW

  1½ **lbs. cubed boneless pork or lamb**
    1 package (⅝ oz.) brown gravy mix
    ½ **teaspoon sugar**
    2 tablespoons all-purpose flour
    1 teaspoon salt
    1 teaspoon Worcestershire sauce
    ⅛ **teaspoon pepper**
    2 cups water*
    6 medium carrots, cut into 1-inch pieces
    2 stalks celery, sliced
    4 medium potatoes, peeled and cut into pieces

1. Combine meat, gravy mix and sugar in 3-quart glass casserole.

2. MICROWAVE, uncovered, 5 minutes. Stir in remaining ingredients.

3. MICROWAVE, covered, 30 to 40 minutes or until meat and vegetables are tender, stirring 2 or 3 times. Let stand 5 minutes.   5 to 6 Servings

TIP • *If desired, use ½ cup wine and 1½ cups water. Red wine goes well with the lamb, white wine with the pork.

Pictured: Beef and Noodle Hot Dish, page 37.

GROUND MEAT REMINDERS

- Grinding tenderizes meat. Beef, pork or lamb in ground form is cooked similarly. Most recipes here call for ground beef, but pork or lamb can also be used.
- Regular ground beef usually has more fat than is desirable in a casserole or sauce. For these dishes the meat is precooked until set and then the fat is drained from the meat. This is also a good time to precook longer-cooking ingredients like onion or celery. This precooking causes the meat to form small chunks just as it does when browned in a frying pan.
- Most ground beef dishes are not cooked long enough to achieve much browning. When the lack of browning is noticeable, as with patties, a sprinkling of gravy mix or the use of the browning element or grill adds a nice brown color and flavor.

The onion soup adds a rich flavor to this meat loaf.

HEARTY MEAT LOAF

   1½ lbs. ground beef
   ⅔ cup milk
   1 egg
   1 envelope onion soup mix
   3 tablespoons brown sugar
   3 tablespoons catsup
   ½ teaspoon prepared mustard

1. Combine ground beef, milk, egg and soup mix; mix well. Press into 8x4 or 9x5-inch glass loaf baking dish. Cover with waxed paper.

2. MICROWAVE 10 minutes (145°), rotating dish once. Drain juices. Combine brown sugar, catsup and mustard; spoon over loaf.

3. MICROWAVE, uncovered, 3 to 5 minutes or until loaf is cooked in center (160°). Let stand a few minutes before serving.   5 to 6 Servings

TIP • *Variable Power:* Microwave medium-high (70%) in step 2 for 15 minutes and in step 3 for 5 to 7 minutes.

A flavorful, moist meat loaf.

FAVORITE MEAT LOAF

   1 lb. ground beef
   ½ lb. bulk pork sausage
   ¾ cup rolled oats (quick or old fashioned)
   1 small onion, chopped
   1 teaspoon salt
   ¼ teaspoon pepper
   ½ cup milk
   1 egg
   ¼ cup catsup

1. Combine all ingredients in mixing bowl; mix well. Press into 9x5 or 8x4-inch glass loaf baking dish. Cover with waxed paper.

2. MICROWAVE 15 to 17 minutes or until just about set in center (160°), rotating dish once or twice. Let stand, covered, 5 minutes before serving.
                                6 to 8 Servings

TIP • *Variable Power:* Microwave medium-high (70%) 20 to 25 minutes.

Like a meat loaf, but served in squares.

SOUPER BEEF SQUARES

   1½ lbs. ground beef
   1 small onion, chopped
   1 egg
   1 teaspoon dried parsley flakes
   ¼ teaspoon salt
   ⅓ cup dry bread crumbs
   1 can (10¾ oz.) condensed cream of mushroom soup
   ¼ cup milk

1. Combine ground beef, onion, egg, parsley, salt, bread crumbs and ½ cup of the soup; mix well. Press into 10x6-inch glass baking dish. Cover with waxed paper.

2. MICROWAVE 11 to 13 minutes or until meat is set in center. Let stand a few minutes. Combine remaining soup and the milk in glass bowl.

3. MICROWAVE, uncovered, 1½ to 2½ minutes or until hot and bubbly. Cut meat mixture into squares and serve with sauce.   4 to 5 Servings

These meatballs simmer right in the sauce. The time is longer to allow the rice to cook.

PORCUPINE MEATBALLS

   1 lb. ground beef
   ¼ cup uncooked long-grain rice
   1 small onion, chopped
   1 teaspoon salt
   ¼ teaspoon pepper
   1 egg
   1 can (10¾ oz.) condensed tomato soup
   1¼ cups water

1. Combine ground beef, rice, onion, salt, pepper and egg. Form into about 24 balls, 1 inch in size. Arrange in shallow 1½-quart glass casserole. Add soup and water.

2. MICROWAVE, covered, 25 to 30 minutes or until rice is tender. If desired, garnish with parsley.

4 to 5 Servings

TIP • With quick-cooking rice, increase amount to ½ cup; reduce water to ¾ cup and cooking time to 15 to 20 minutes.

Meatballs are precooked to remove the excess fat and help hold their shape.

SWEDISH MEATBALLS

   1 lb. ground beef
   1 small onion, chopped
   1 egg
   ¼ cup dry bread crumbs
   2 tablespoons milk
   ½ teaspoon salt
   ⅛ teaspoon pepper
Sauce
   1 can (10¾ oz.) condensed cream of chicken soup
   ⅓ cup sour cream
   ¼ cup milk
   1 tablespoon dried parsley flakes
   ⅛ teaspoon nutmeg

1. Combine ground beef, onion, egg, crumbs, milk, salt and pepper; mix well. Form into about 24 meatballs, 1 inch in size. Arrange in shallow 1½-quart glass casserole.

2. MICROWAVE, uncovered, 6 to 7 minutes or until meat is set; drain fat. Combine sauce ingredients; pour over meatballs.

3. MICROWAVE, covered, 5 to 6 minutes or until hot and bubbly. If desired, serve with rice or potatoes.

4 to 5 Servings

Use gravy mix or a browning grill to develop rich color on meats that cook quickly.

FAVORITE MEAT PATTIES

   1½ lbs. ground beef
   1 small onion, chopped
   2 slices bread, cubed
   ⅓ cup milk
   ¼ cup catsup
   1 teaspoon salt
   2 teaspoons Worcestershire sauce
   1 teaspoon prepared mustard
   Brown gravy mix

1. Combine all ingredients except gravy mix; mix well. Shape into 6 patties; place in ungreased 12x8-inch glass baking dish. Sprinkle lightly with gravy mix. Cover with waxed paper.

2. MICROWAVE 7 to 8 minutes or until desired doneness.   6 Patties

TIPS • A microwave roasting rack can be used in the baking dish to keep the patties above the cooking juices.

   • Sprinkle-on browning seasonings can be substituted for gravy mix.

   • *Browning Element:* Omit gravy mix. Place shelf in upper position. Microwave high 4 minutes, rotating dish once. Turn patties over. Brown 5 to 7 minutes, rotating dish once.

Green peppers are simple to prepare with the microwave oven. The corn and peppers make these especially colorful. Pictured on cover.

CORN AND BEEF-STUFFED PEPPERS

4 medium green peppers
1 lb. ground beef
1 egg
½ cup quick-cooking rice
1 teaspoon salt
⅛ teaspoon pepper
1 can (8 oz.) tomato sauce
1 can (7 oz.) whole kernel corn, drained
About ½ cup catsup or barbecue sauce

1. Cut peppers in half lengthwise; remove core and seeds. Place cut-side-up in 12x8-inch or 13x9-inch glass baking dish.
2. Crumble beef into medium bowl; mix in egg. Stir in remaining ingredients except catsup. Fill pepper halves with mixture. Top each with about 1 tablespoon catsup. Cover with waxed paper.
3. MICROWAVE 12 to 14 minutes or until meat is done (150°).

4 to 6 Servings

TIP • This method gives a tender crisp green pepper. For a softer texture, cover the peppers in step 1 with waxed paper and microwave 3 to 4 minutes or until heated through. Continue with steps 2 and 3.

Ham, apple and stuffing — a flavorful combination. If desired, serve with a cheese or white sauce.

HAM AND STUFFING CASSEROLE

1 package (6 oz.) saucepan stuffing mix
2 cups ground or finely chopped cooked ham
1 medium apple, peeled and chopped
1¾ cups milk
3 eggs
2 tablespoons butter or margarine

1. Combine stuffing mix (with seasonings), ham and apple in 8-inch square glass baking dish.

2. Combine milk and eggs; pour over stuffing, mixing until well combined. Cut butter into pieces; place on stuffing mixture. Cover with waxed paper.
3. MICROWAVE 12 to 15 minutes or until knife inserted near center comes out clean (150°), rotating dish once. Serve cut into squares.

5 to 6 Servings

TIP • *Variable Power:* Microwave medium-high (70%) 14 to 16 minutes.

The microwave time for this recipe is determined by the time needed to cook the rice.

BEEF AND RICE CASSEROLE

1 lb. ground beef
1 medium onion, chopped
1 can (10¾ oz.) condensed cream of celery soup
1 cup uncooked long-grain rice
1 cup milk
1½ cups water
1 tablespoon Worcestershire sauce
½ teaspoon salt
½ cup sliced stuffed green olives

1. Crumble ground beef into 2½ or 3-quart glass casserole; add onion.
2. MICROWAVE, uncovered, 5 to 6 minutes or until meat is set. Stir to break meat into pieces; drain fat. Stir in remaining ingredients.
3. MICROWAVE, covered, 25 to 30 minutes or until rice is tender, stirring 2 or 3 times. Let stand several minutes before serving.   5 to 6 Servings

TIP • *Variable Power:* In step 3, microwave high 10 to 12 minutes or until mixture boils, Then, microwave low (30%) 22 to 25 minutes.

The uncooked noodles cook right along with the other casserole ingredients. Pictured on page 33.

BEEF AND NOODLE HOT DISH

1 lb. ground beef
1 medium onion, chopped
1 stalk celery, chopped
1 can (16 oz.) tomatoes, undrained
1 can (16 oz.) whole kernel corn, undrained
⅓ cup water
½ cup catsup
1 teaspoon salt
1 teaspoon chili powder
⅛ teaspoon pepper
2 cups uncooked noodles

1. Crumble ground beef into 2½ or 3-quart glass casserole; add onion and celery.

2. MICROWAVE, covered, 6 to 7 minutes or until celery is tender. Stir to break meat into pieces; drain fat. Stir in remaining ingredients.

3. MICROWAVE, covered, 15 to 18 minutes or until noodles are tender, stirring 2 or 3 times. Let stand several minutes before serving.

5 to 6 Servings

This recipe has been popular in class.

GROUND BEEF STROGANOFF

1 lb. ground beef
1 small onion, chopped
½ teaspoon instant beef bouillon
1 can (10¾ oz.) condensed cream of mushroom soup
¼ cup water
½ cup sour cream

1. Crumble ground beef into 1½-quart glass casserole; add onion.

2. MICROWAVE, uncovered, 5 to 6 minutes or until meat is set. Stir to break meat into pieces; drain fat. Stir in remaining ingredients.

3. MICROWAVE, covered, 7 to 8 minutes or until heated through. If desired, serve over rice or noodles.

4 to 5 Servings

A spicy, layered casserole that only needs heating.

MEXICAN BEEF AND CHIP CASSEROLE

1 lb. ground beef
1 small onion, chopped
1 clove garlic, minced
1 can (10¾ oz.) condensed cream of mushroom soup
1 can (4 oz.) chopped green chilies
1 package (6¼ oz.) corn or tortilla chips
1 can (10 oz.) mild enchilada sauce
2 cups shredded Monterey Jack cheese

1. Crumble ground beef into 1-quart glass casserole; add onion and garlic.

2. MICROWAVE, uncovered, 5 to 6 minutes or until meat is set. Stir to break meat into pieces; drain fat. Stir in soup and chilies.

3. Layer ⅓ (about 2 cups) corn chips and half each of meat mixture, enchilada sauce and cheese in 12x8-inch glass baking dish. Top with another third of corn chips and remaining meat mixture, enchilada sauce and cheese. Sprinkle with remaining corn chips.

4. MICROWAVE, uncovered, 10 to 12 minutes or until hot and bubbly (155°).

6 to 8 Servings

TIPS • If chopping whole chilies, be sure to discard the seeds as they are very hot.

• *Variable Power:* In step 4, microwave medium-high (70%) 14 to 16 minutes.

Eggs and Cheese

ABOUT EGGS AND CHEESE: Both eggs and cheese are sensitive to overcooking. When eggs are overcooked they become tough and rubbery; when cheese is overcooked, it becomes tough and stringy.

Egg yolks, which are high in fat, cook more quickly than the whites, which have no fat. This difference is eliminated when the eggs are mixed together as for scrambled eggs. When the eggs are cooked without mixing, either a lower power setting or an added ingredient such as water is necessary to slow the cooking. For traditional fried eggs, a hot browning grill is used as an auxiliary source of cooking.

Recipes for omelets and soufflés are not included here. Omelets can be cooked, but they must be stirred to prevent the outside edges from overcooking before the center is done. The result is somewhat like scrambled eggs. Soufflés need dry oven heat to crust and hold their puffy shape.

Cheese is added to a dish at the beginning when the dish is cooking only to heat through. If the dish will cook longer than this, it is best to add the cheese near the end of the cooking time. This will prevent it from becoming tough and rubbery.

The hot grill or skillet helps cook the egg whites while microwaves quickly cook the yolks.

SUNNY-SIDE-UP EGGS

1. MICROWAVE a browning grill or skillet 3 minutes to preheat.
2. Spread a small amount butter or bacon drippings on grill to coat lightly. Break 1 to 4 eggs onto hot grill.
3. MICROWAVE, uncovered, until eggs are desired doneness:
   - 1 egg — 1 to 1½ minutes
   - 2 to 4 eggs — 1¼ to 1¾ minutes

TIP • If you do not have a browning grill or skillet, use a glass ceramic frying pan and preheat it on a burner over medium-high heat. Add eggs and microwave as directed.

Pictured: Quiche Lorraine, page 41.

SCRAMBLED EGGS

1. Combine eggs and milk (1 tablespoon per egg) in glass casserole or dish; mix with fork until blended. Add 1 teaspoon butter per egg.
2. MICROWAVE, covered, until eggs are set, yet moist, stirring twice during last half of cooking time:
   - 1 egg — ¾ to 1 minute
   - 2 eggs — 1¼ to 1½ minutes
   - 4 eggs — 2½ to 3 minutes
   - 6 eggs — 3½ to 4 minutes
   - 8 eggs — 4 to 4½ minutes
3. Let stand a few minutes; season to taste with salt and pepper.

TIP • *Variable Power:* With 1 egg microwave medium-high (70%) 1 to 1½ minutes; 2 eggs 1½ to 2 minutes and 4 eggs 3½ to 4 minutes. For larger quantities, use high setting.

Try this for a supper or luncheon. The flavor combination is delicious.

ORIENTAL SCRAMBLED EGGS

   ¼ **cup butter or margarine**
   1 **cup sliced fresh mushrooms**
   ¼ **cup sliced green onion**
   6 **eggs, beaten**
   1 **can (5 oz.) boned chicken, cut up**
   1 **tablespoon soy sauce**
   ⅛ **teaspoon ginger**
   Hot cooked rice

1. Combine butter, mushrooms and onion in 1-quart glass casserole.
2. MICROWAVE, covered, 4 to 5 minutes or until vegetables are tender.
3. Stir in eggs, chicken, 1 tablespoon soy sauce, and the ginger.
4. MICROWAVE, covered, 3½ to 4½ minutes or until eggs are set, yet moist, stirring twice during last half of cooking time. Serve with rice and additional soy sauce.   4 to 5 Servings

TIP • When using leftover cooked chicken, use ¾ cup finely chopped chicken and ¼ cup chicken broth.

EGG REMINDERS
• Do not try to cook eggs in the shell. Pressure will build up inside the egg, causing it to explode.
• Eggs need stirring or slow cooking to prevent overcooking some areas before other parts reach the desired doneness. Most egg dishes are cooked covered to hold in the heat.
• Yolks and whites cook at different rates. Scrambling minimizes this difference. Otherwise, cook with water to slow the cooking or use an additional source of heat such as a browning grill.

This makes a good casserole for a meatless supper — potatoes, spinach, cheese and eggs.

EGGS FLORENTINE STYLE

> **2 packages (10 ozs. each) frozen chopped spinach**
> **1 package (12 oz.) frozen hash browns**
> **2 tablespoons chopped onion**
> **1 tablespoon lemon juice**
> **Cheese Sauce, page 65**
> **8 eggs**
> **2 tablespoons butter or margarine**
> **⅓ cup dry bread crumbs**

1. MICROWAVE spinach and potatoes in packages 9 to 10 minutes or until thawed; drain spinach well. Combine spinach, potatoes, onion and lemon juice in 12x8-inch glass baking dish.
2. Prepare cheese sauce as directed; pour hot sauce over spinach mixture. Make 8 indentations in spinach mixture; break an egg into each.
3. MICROWAVE butter in small dish about ½ minute or until melted. Stir in bread crumbs; sprinkle over eggs. Cover with waxed paper.
4. MICROWAVE 10 to 12 minutes or until eggs are just about set, rotating dish once. Let stand a few minutes; season to taste with salt and pepper.

4 to 6 Servings

TIP • *Variable Power:* In step 4, microwave medium-high (70%) for 12 minutes. Then, microwave high 1 to 2 minutes.

The addition of water slows and evens the cooking. Without water, one egg cooks in about ½ minute, but it may also be overcooked in areas.

BAKED EGGS

1. Place an egg in each buttered 5 or 6-oz. glass custard cup. Sprinkle with salt and pepper. If desired, add 1 teaspoon cream or milk to each cup. Set cups in 9-inch glass pie plate. Add 1 cup warm water to pie plate. Cover eggs with plastic wrap.
2. MICROWAVE until eggs are desired doneness:

> 1 egg — 1½ to 2 minutes
> 2 eggs — 2 to 3 minutes
> 4 eggs — 3 to 4 minutes
> 6 eggs — 4 to 5 minutes

TIP • When cooking 2 or more eggs, it may be necessary to rotate the dish once for even cooking.

Ham, green pepper and tomato give these scrambled eggs their "Denver" flavor. Good for brunch or as a sandwich filling.

DENVER SCRAMBLED EGGS

> **8 eggs**
> **½ cup milk**
> **½ cup salad dressing or mayonnaise**
> **¼ cup chopped pimiento**
> **¼ cup chopped green pepper**
> **1 cup cubed cooked ham**
> **½ teaspoon salt**
> **1 medium tomato, cut into pieces**
> **6 to 8 slices toast or toasted English muffins**

1. Beat together eggs, milk and salad dressing in 1½ or 2-quart glass casserole. Stir in pimiento, green pepper, ham and salt.
2. MICROWAVE, covered, 4 to 5 minutes or until just about set, stirring twice during last half of cooking time. Stir in tomato. Let stand a few minutes before serving on toast.

6 to 8 Servings

CHEESE REMINDERS
• Avoid overcooking as this makes cheese tough and stringy.
• Select the flavor of cheese according to personal preferences and other flavors in the dish. Processed cheese melts to a creamier consistency and is more tolerant of overcooking than natural cheese. However, there is a definite difference in flavor between natural and processed cheese.

In this recipe, extra water is added so that the macaroni cooks along with the sauce.

ONE-STEP MACARONI 'N CHEESE

  1½ **cups uncooked macaroni**
    1 **small onion, chopped**
  1½ **tablespoons all-purpose flour**
    1 **tablespoon chopped pimiento**
    1 **teaspoon salt**
  ½ **teaspoon Worcestershire sauce**
  1½ **cups water**
    1 **cup milk**
    2 **tablespoons butter or margarine**
    1 **cup cubed or shredded cheese**

1. Combine all ingredients except cheese in 2 or 2½-quart glass casserole.
2. MICROWAVE, covered, 5 to 7 minutes or until mixture boils. Let stand 5 minutes. Add cheese.
3. MICROWAVE 2 to 3 minutes or until mixture boils and thickens. Let stand several minutes before serving.
                          5 to 6 Servings
TIP • *Variable Power:* In step 2, microwave high 5 to 7 minutes or until mixture boils. Then, microwave low (30%) 9 to 10 minutes or until tender. Add cheese and complete step 3.

Here the macaroni and sauce are cooked separately, then combined with the cheese.

TWO-STEP MACARONI 'N CHEESE

  1½ **cups uncooked macaroni**
    3 **tablespoons butter or margarine**
    2 **tablespoons chopped onion**
    3 **tablespoons all-purpose flour**
  1½ **cups milk**
    1 **teaspoon salt**
    Dash pepper
    Dash Tabasco sauce
    1 **cup chopped tomato**
  1½ **cups cubed or shredded**
      Cheddar or American cheese
  ½ **cup crushed potato chips**

1. Cook macaroni as directed on package; drain.
2. MICROWAVE butter and onion in uncovered 1½ or 2-quart glass casserole 2 to 3 minutes or until onion is limp. Blend in flour; stir in milk, salt, pepper and Tabasco sauce.
3. MICROWAVE, uncovered, 4 to 5 minutes or until mixture boils, stirring occasionally during last half of cooking time. Stir in tomato, cheese and cooked macaroni; sprinkle with potato chips.
4. MICROWAVE, uncovered, 4 to 6 minutes or until heated through.
                          5 to 6 Servings

This cooks similarly to custard pies. The crust is precooked before the filling is added. A browning element or broiler adds a golden touch the last minutes. Pictured on page 38.

QUICHE LORRAINE

   10 **slices bacon**
    9-inch **baked pastry shell**
  1½ **cups shredded Swiss cheese**
  1½ **cups light cream or evaporated milk**
    3 **eggs**
  ¼ **teaspoon salt**
  ⅛ **teaspoon pepper**
    1 **tablespoon chopped chives**

1. Arrange bacon in layers on glass plate or in baking dish. Cover with paper towel.
2. MICROWAVE 5½ to 7 minutes or until crisp; set aside.
3. Prepare pastry shell in glass pie plate or quiche pan. Crumble bacon and add with cheese to pastry shell.
4. MICROWAVE cream in 2-cup glass measure 3 to 4 minutes or until hot. Beat eggs and remaining ingredients; beat in hot milk. Pour into pastry shell.
5. MICROWAVE high 5 minutes. Rotate dish once. Microwave medium (50%) 8 to 10 minutes or until just about set. Let stand a few minutes before cutting.

TIP • *Browning Element:* After microwaving, place quiche 3 inches from element. Brown 12 to 15 minutes, rotating dish once.

Soups and Sandwiches

ABOUT SOUPS: Some soups are prepared from a combination of cooked ingredients. They need to be heated just until steaming hot and flavors are blended. Allow about 2 minutes for each cup of soup being heated.

Other soups contain ingredients that require cooking. These particular ingredients determine the cooking time for the soups.

Covering speeds the heating or cooking of any soup. A casserole cover, an overturned plate, or a piece of plastic wrap or waxed paper may be used. With some tall narrow-topped containers, the covering can be omitted. Since the opening is very small, the lack of covering has little effect on the cooking time required.

Because of the dehydrated ingredients in these mixes, the hot soup needs to stand several minutes before serving.

SOUP MIXES

1. Prepare 1 envelope soup mix in 4-cup glass measure, using amount of water directed on package.
2. MICROWAVE, covered, 3 to 4 minutes or until mixture comes to a boil. Let stand, covered, at least 5 minutes before serving.

3 to 4 Servings

Pictured: Bacon, Cheese and Tomato Sandwiches, page 46, and Ham and Cheese Chowder, page 44.

SOUP REMINDERS
• When heating, allow about 2 minutes for each cup of soup.
• Covering speeds heating; stir the soup either during the heating time or just before serving.
• Soup flavors usually improve upon standing. When convenient, make the soup ahead, then just reheat in the bowls at serving time.

A popular favorite. For best flavor, make ahead and reheat for serving.

CHILI

    1 lb. ground beef
    1 medium onion, chopped
    1 medium green pepper, chopped
    1 can (28 oz.) tomatoes,
      undrained
    1 can (15½ oz.) kidney beans,
      undrained
    2 to 3 teaspoons chili powder
    1 teaspoon salt
    ⅛ teaspoon cayenne pepper

1. Crumble ground beef into 2-quart glass casserole; add onion.
2. MICROWAVE, uncovered, 5 to 6 minutes or until meat is set. Stir to break meat into pieces; drain fat. Stir in remaining ingredients.
3. MICROWAVE, covered, 12 to 15 minutes or until flavors are blended.

5 to 6 Servings

This simple-to-fix soup is even easier with a microwave oven.

SOUP MIXES (FOR CUP SERVINGS)

1. Combine envelope of soup for a cup mix and water in large glass cup or mug.
2. MICROWAVE, uncovered, 1½ to 2 minutes or until hot, stirring once.

1 Serving

A classic soup that adapts well to microwave cooking.

FRENCH ONION SOUP

    3 medium onions, chopped
    ¼ cup butter or margarine
    2 tablespoons instant beef
       bouillon
    2 tablespoons soy sauce
    1 tablespoon Worcestershire
       sauce
    ½ teaspoon paprika
    Dash pepper
    5 cups water

1. Combine onions and butter in 3-quart glass casserole.

2. MICROWAVE, covered, 9 to 11 minutes or until onions are tender, stirring once. Stir in remaining ingredients.

3. MICROWAVE, covered, 8 to 10 minutes or until hot.   5 to 6 Servings

TIP • If desired, broil slices of French bread until golden brown. Sprinkle with shredded Swiss cheese; broil until cheese is melted. Top each bowl of soup with a slice.

A smooth and creamy soup with bits of ham. Processed cheese is best for the creamy consistency desired. Pictured on page 42.

HAM AND CHEESE CHOWDER

    2 stalks celery, chopped
    1 medium onion, chopped
    3 tablespoons butter or margarine
    3 tablespoons all-purpose flour
    ¼ teaspoon salt
    3 cups milk
    2 cups (8 ozs.) cubed cooked
       ham
  1½ cups shredded processed
       American cheese

1. Combine celery, onion and butter in 3-quart glass casserole.

2. MICROWAVE, covered, 5 to 6 minutes or until vegetables are tender, stirring once. Stir in flour, salt and milk.

3. MICROWAVE, covered, 7 to 8 minutes or until mixture boils, stirring once or twice. Add ham and cheese.

4. MICROWAVE, covered, 4 to 5 minutes or until cheese is melted.
                    5 to 6 Servings

A hearty clam chowder. If desired, leftover cooked fish can be added along with clams.

CLAM CHOWDER

    3 slices bacon
    1 can (8 oz.) minced clams
    2 medium potatoes, peeled and
       cubed
    1 small onion, chopped
    2 medium carrots, sliced
  2½ cups milk
    3 tablespoons all-purpose flour
    1 tablespoon dried parsley flakes
    ½ teaspoon salt
    Dash pepper

1. Arrange bacon in 2-quart glass casserole. Cover with paper towel.

2. MICROWAVE 2½ to 2¾ minutes or until crisp. Remove bacon and set aside. Drain clam liquid into drippings. Add potatoes, onion and carrots.

3. MICROWAVE, covered, 8 to 10 minutes or until vegetables are tender, stirring once. Combine milk and flour; add to vegetables along with clams and remaining ingredients.

4. MICROWAVE, covered, 5 to 6 minutes or until mixture boils, stirring once. Crumble bacon and use to garnish soup.   4 to 5 Servings

Ground beef makes a quick starter for a hearty beef and vegetable soup.

GROUND BEEF-VEGETABLE SOUP

1 lb. ground beef
1 envelope onion soup mix
1 can (16 oz.) tomatoes,
  undrained
2 cups uncooked noodles
4 cups water
1 bay leaf
1 teaspoon salt
⅛ teaspoon pepper
1 package (10 oz.) frozen mixed
  vegetables

1. Crumble ground beef into 3-quart glass casserole.
2. MICROWAVE, uncovered, 5 to 6 minutes or until meat is set. Stir to break meat into pieces; drain fat. Stir in remaining ingredients.
3. MICROWAVE, covered, 20 to 25 minutes or until mixture boils and noodles are tender. Remove bay leaf before serving.   8 to 10 Servings

This chowder was a special favorite of our home tester.

SAUSAGE-CORN CHOWDER

1 lb. link pork sausages
1 medium onion, chopped
1 small green pepper, chopped
2 medium potatoes, peeled and
  cubed
1 cup water
1 can (16 oz.) cream-style corn
2 cups milk
2 tablespoons all-purpose flour
½ teaspoon salt
Dash pepper
2 tablespoons chopped pimiento

1. MICROWAVE sausages in uncovered 2½ or 3-quart glass casserole 6 to 7 minutes or until no longer pink, rearranging once. Drain all but 1 tablespoon drippings. Cut sausages into pieces. Add onion, green pepper, potatoes and water.
2. MICROWAVE, covered, 10 to 12 minutes or until vegetables are tender. Add corn. Combine milk, flour, salt and pepper; add to casserole along with pimiento.

3. MICROWAVE, covered, 7 to 9 minutes or until mixture boils, stirring once or twice.   6 to 8 Servings

Both macaroni and cabbage cook fairly quickly and will cook while the mixture heats.

SPEEDY MINESTRONE

2 cups cubed cooked beef, pork
  or poultry
1 can (16 oz.) tomatoes,
  undrained
1 can (10¾ oz.) condensed
  tomato soup
1 can (15½ oz.) kidney beans,
  undrained
½ cup uncooked macaroni
2 cups shredded cabbage
1 cup water
1 tablespoon Worcestershire
  sauce
½ teaspoon salt
½ teaspoon garlic salt
¼ teaspoon pepper

1. Combine all ingredients in 3-quart glass casserole.
2. MICROWAVE, covered, 20 to 25 minutes or until macaroni is tender, stirring once or twice. If desired, sprinkle individual servings with Parmesan cheese.   8 to 10 Servings

Heat soup right in the serving bowl.

CANNED SOUPS

1. Divide contents from 10¾-oz. can favorite condensed soup between 2 or 3 glass bowls. Add equal amounts of water; stir to combine. Cover each bowl with small glass plate.
2. MICROWAVE 3½ to 4½ minutes or until edges are bubbly. Stir before serving.   2 to 3 Servings

TIPS • For one bowl, microwave
   2 to 3 minutes.
      • For four bowls (2 cans of soup),
   microwave 6 to 7 minutes.

ABOUT SANDWICHES: Sandwiches heat very quickly. Since bread is porous and the filling is usually more dense, the filling determines the heating time necessary. Often sandwiches are overheated giving the bread a tough, rubbery texture. To help prevent this, use several thin-cut slices of filling rather than one thick slice, and heat just until you see steam when the top of the bun is lifted.

Sandwiches with the same type filling will heat in the same time whether the filling is sandwiched between two slices bread or served open-faced.

Since the filling always takes the longest to heat, a frozen roll can be used without affecting the timing or end product. However, do not use a frozen filling unless it is first thawed before placing in the bread.

When sandwiches heat, the moisture in the bread comes to the outside. This moisture needs to be able to escape into the air and evaporate. If it is trapped between a tight fitting cover or plate and the bread or roll, the crust will become soggy. Paper plates, napkins or towels are often used for sandwiches because they allow the moisture to escape, yet hold in some of the heat.

Thin slices of meat heat quickly. One thick slice would take longer and overcook the bread before the meat is hot.

SLICED MEAT OR POULTRY SANDWICHES

1. Place 3 or 4 thin slices cooked meat or poultry in each split sandwich or hamburger bun. If desired, top meat with 1 tablespoon sandwich spread or barbecue sauce. Place on paper plate, napkin or towel.
2. MICROWAVE until filling steams when top of bun is lifted:

1 sandwich	— ½ to 1	minute
2 sandwiches	— 1 to 1½	minutes
4 sandwiches	— 2 to 3	minutes
6 sandwiches	— 3 to 4	minutes

Let stand a minute or two before serving.

The microwave oven cooks the bacon and heats the completed sandwiches. Pictured on page 42.

BACON, CHEESE AND TOMATO SANDWICHES

    5 slices bacon
    5 slices bread, toasted
  ¼ cup mayonnaise or salad dressing
    2 medium tomatoes, sliced
    5 slices Swiss, Cheddar or American cheese

1. Arrange bacon between layers of paper towels in shallow glass baking dish.
2. MICROWAVE 3½ to 4 minutes or until crisp; set aside.
3. Arrange toast on paper-lined glass platter. Spread each piece with mayonnaise. Top with tomato and cheese slices. Crumble a slice of bacon onto each sandwich.
4. MICROWAVE, uncovered, 2 to 2½ minutes or until cheese is melted.
                            5 Sandwiches

Crabmeat and tomato slices served open-faced on English muffins.

HOT CRABMEAT SANDWICHES

    1 package (3 oz.) cream cheese with chives
    2 tablespoons chopped onion
    2 tablespoons mayonnaise or salad dressing
  ½ tablespoon lemon juice
    1 can (7 oz.) crabmeat, drained
    4 English muffins, split and toasted
    2 tomatoes, sliced
    Paprika

1. MICROWAVE cream cheese in glass bowl ¼ to ½ minute or until softened. Mix in onion, mayonnaise, lemon juice and crabmeat.
2. Arrange English muffins cut-side-up on paper-lined glass plate. Top muffins with tomato slices and crab mixture. Sprinkle with paprika.
3. MICROWAVE, uncovered, 2½ to 3 minutes or until filling is warm.
                            8 Sandwiches

SANDWICH REMINDERS
• The filling determines the heating time and will always be hotter than the bread feels.
• Don't overheat as that makes the bread chewy and tough.
• Place sandwiches on paper or cloth to absorb any moisture from the bread. It can be a paper plate or a napkin-lined glass plate.
• Toasted bread and buns are less apt to become soggy than if untoasted.
• Frozen bread or rolls can be used for sandwiches, but avoid using frozen fillings unless they are first thawed.

HOT DOGS
1. Place a wiener in each split hot dog bun. Arrange on paper plate, napkin or towel.
2. MICROWAVE until wiener feels warm:
    1 hot dog — ½ to ¾ minute
    2 hot dogs — ¾ to 1 minute
    4 hot dogs — 1¼ to 1½ minutes
    6 hot dogs — 1¾ to 2 minutes
Let stand a minute or two before serving.

Tuna and cheese, served on hamburger buns.

OPEN-FACED TUNA BUNS
    1 can (6½ oz.) tuna fish, drained
    1 cup cubed American or Cheddar cheese
    ⅓ cup mayonnaise or salad dressing
    ¼ cup chopped sweet or dill pickle
    2 tablespoons chopped green onion
    ½ teaspoon prepared mustard
    4 hamburger buns, split
    Sliced green olives
1. Combine all ingredients except buns and olives; mix well. Arrange buns cut-side-up on paper plate, towel or napkin. Spread with tuna mixture; garnish with olives.
2. MICROWAVE, uncovered, 2 to 2½ minutes or until cheese begins to melt.
8 Sandwiches

For browning these patties, a preheated grill is used.

HAMBURGERS
1. Season 1 lb. ground beef with salt and pepper. Shape into 4 patties.
2. MICROWAVE browning grill about 5 minutes to preheat. Place patties on grill.
3. MICROWAVE, uncovered, ½ minute. Turn patties over.
4. MICROWAVE, uncovered, 1½ to 2 minutes or until desired doneness.
5. MICROWAVE 4 buns on paper plate or towel 1 to 1½ minutes or until warm. Place a hamburger patty in each. Top with mayonnaise, lettuce and tomato or other favorite hamburger topping. 4 Hamburgers

TIP • The Favorite Meat Patties recipe, page 35, can also be used for Hamburgers.

This Sloppy Joe filling contains a surprise ingredient — cabbage. It is a tasty, nutritious addition.

SLOPPY JOES
    1 lb. ground beef
    1 small onion, chopped
    ½ cup chopped green pepper
    2 cups shredded cabbage
    1 can (8 oz.) tomato sauce
    1 teaspoon salt
    1 teaspoon prepared mustard
    1 tablespoon brown sugar
    6 to 8 hamburger buns, split
1. Crumble ground beef into 1½-quart glass casserole; add onion.
2. MICROWAVE, uncovered, 5 to 6 minutes or until meat is set. Stir to break meat into pieces; drain fat. Stir in remaining ingredients except buns.
3. MICROWAVE, covered, 14 to 16 minutes or until cabbage is desired doneness, stirring once or twice. Spoon onto bottom halves of buns arranged on glass plate. Top with other half of buns.
4. MICROWAVE, uncovered, 1 to 2 minutes or until buns are warm.
6 to 8 Sandwiches

Vegetables

ABOUT VEGETABLES: Most vegetables cook to perfection in the microwave oven. They retain a delightful tender-crisp texture with picture pretty color.

Since microwave cooking is like steaming, very little additional liquid is needed. Covering speeds the cooking of most vegetables.

Dried vegetables like beans and peas require long, slow simmering to become tender. This slow cooking can be achieved with a slow simmer setting, but there will be little if any time savings.

Some recipes in this chapter call for fresh vegetables while others require frozen vegetables. The two types are usually interchangeable with very little adjustment in cooking time. Fresh vegetables need a little water or butter added for moisture during cooking while frozen vegetables normally do not require additional moisture.

FRESH VEGETABLE REMINDERS
• Add 1 to 2 tablespoons water to most fresh vegetables and cook in a covered casserole. This moisture can also be in the form of cream or butter.
• **Most fresh vegetables require 6 to 9 minutes cooking time** for 4 to 6 servings. Vegetables that are finely cut like shredded cabbage may require slightly less time and vegetables that are in larger pieces like broccoli spears may require slightly longer time.
• Vegetables like potatoes and squash have a peeling that is often left on during cooking. This serves the same purpose as a casserole with a tight-fitting cover.

FROZEN VEGETABLE REMINDERS
• **One package of frozen vegetables usually requires 6 to 9 minutes cooking time** to thaw and heat. For 2 packages, allow 10 to 13 minutes cooking time.
• Frozen vegetables cook best in a covered container. Usually there is enough moisture on the frozen vegetable without adding additional water.
• When thawing a vegetable to add to another dish, leave it in the paper packaging. You may wish to remove the outer waxed paper so that the ink does not melt onto the oven surface, or just place the package on a paper towel.
• About 1½ cups of the bulk-pack frozen vegetables equals an 8 to 10-oz. package.
• Frozen vegetables packaged in plastic cooking pouches can be cooked right in that pouch. Just be sure to pierce a small hole on the top side so that the steam can escape. Use the same 6 to 9 minute cooking time per package as a guide.

CANNED VEGETABLE REMINDERS
• These vegetables are cooked during the canning process so only need to be heated to serving temperature. Allow about 2 minutes heating time for each cup of vegetable.
• Vegetables can be heated right in the serving dish. Use an overturned plate or waxed paper if the dish lacks a cover.
• The canning liquid can either be left on the vegetable or drained before heating. Add seasonings after heating.

Pictured: Peas and Onions, page 54.

Try the tangy sauce on cauliflower and broccoli, too.

ASPARAGUS WITH TANGY CREAM SAUCE

> 2 packages (8 or 10 ozs. each) frozen cut asparagus
> 1/3 cup mayonnaise or salad dressing
> 1 teaspoon dried parsley flakes
> 1/2 teaspoon onion salt
> 1/2 teaspoon prepared mustard

1. MICROWAVE asparagus in covered 1½-quart glass casserole 10 to 12 minutes or until tender. Drain. Combine remaining ingredients; add to asparagus. Mix lightly just until asparagus is coated.

2. MICROWAVE, uncovered, 1 to 2 minutes or until hot.   6 to 8 Servings

TIP • For fresh asparagus, use 1½ lbs. and add 1 tablespoon water when cooking in step 1.

Use the times in step 1 for toasting almonds for other uses, too.

GREEN BEANS WITH TOASTED ALMONDS

> 2 tablespoons butter or margarine
> 3 tablespoons slivered almonds
> 2 packages (9 or 10 ozs. each) frozen French-cut green beans
> 1 can (6 oz.) water chestnuts, drained and sliced
> 2 tablespoons soy sauce

1. MICROWAVE butter and almonds in uncovered 1½-quart glass casserole 4 to 5 minutes or until almonds are toasted, stirring occasionally; set aside.

2. MICROWAVE beans in packages 8 minutes. Drain any liquid. Add beans to toasted almonds. Stir in water chestnuts and soy sauce.

3. MICROWAVE, covered, 6 to 7 minutes or until heated through.
     6 to 8 Servings

The beans and seasonings are cooked separately so the excess liquid can be drained from the beans.

GREEN BEANS 'N BACON

> 2 slices bacon, cut into pieces
> 2 green onions, sliced
> 1 tablespoon vinegar
> 1 teaspoon dill weed
> 1/2 teaspoon sugar
> 1/4 teaspoon salt
> 1 package (9 or 10 oz.) frozen French-cut green beans

1. Combine bacon and onions in 1-quart glass casserole.

2. MICROWAVE, uncovered, 2 to 2½ minutes or until bacon is crisp. Add vinegar, dill weed, sugar and salt; set aside.

3. MICROWAVE beans in package 6 to 7 minutes or until just about done. Drain if necessary. Add to mixture in casserole; toss lightly to season evenly.

4. MICROWAVE, uncovered, 1 to 2 minutes or until heated through.
     3 to 4 Servings

An easy-to-do, delicious tasting combination.

THREE-BEAN BAKE

> 1 can (31 oz.) pork and beans in tomato sauce
> 1 can (16 oz.) cut green beans, drained
> 1 can (15 oz.) garbanzo beans or chick peas, drained
> 1 small onion, chopped
> 3 tablespoons brown sugar
> 1 tablespoon prepared mustard
> 1/4 cup catsup
> 3 slices bacon, cut into pieces

1. Combine all ingredients except bacon in 2-quart glass casserole. Top with bacon.

2. MICROWAVE, covered, 14 to 16 minutes or until heated through.
     8 to 10 Servings

This sour cream-poppy seed topping goes well with fresh or frozen broccoli.

COUNTRY-STYLE BROCCOLI

**2 packages (10 ozs. each) frozen
  broccoli spears
2 tablespoons chopped onion
½ cup sour cream
1 teaspoon sugar
½ teaspoon poppy seed
½ teaspoon salt**

1. Combine broccoli and onion in 1½ or 2-quart glass casserole.
2. MICROWAVE 11 to 13 minutes or until desired doneness, rearranging once; drain. Combine remaining ingredients; spoon over broccoli.
3. MICROWAVE, uncovered, ½ to 1 minute or until heated through.

6 to 8 Servings

TIP • For fresh broccoli, use 1½ lbs. and add 1 tablespoon water in step 1.

Our home tester really enjoyed the fresh Brussels sprouts cooked in the microwave oven.

BRUSSELS SPROUTS WITH LEMON BUTTER

**1 lb. (4 cups) fresh Brussels
  sprouts
1 tablespoon water
2 tablespoons butter or margarine
½ tablespoon lemon juice
¼ teaspoon salt
1 tablespoon grated Parmesan
  cheese**

1. Combine Brussels sprouts and water in 1½-quart glass casserole.
2. MICROWAVE, covered, 8 to 9 minutes or until just about tender; drain if necessary. Add butter.
3. MICROWAVE, covered, about 1 minute to melt butter. Stir in lemon juice and salt. Sprinkle with Parmesan cheese. Let stand a few minutes before serving.   4 to 5 Servings

Butter provides the moisture and seasoning for cooking this cabbage.

BUTTERED CABBAGE

**4 cups (½ med. head) shredded
  cabbage
2 tablespoons butter or margarine
Salt and pepper**

1. Combine cabbage and butter in 1½-quart glass casserole.
2. MICROWAVE, covered, 6 to 8 minutes or until cabbage is desired doneness, stirring once. Season with salt and pepper.   5 to 6 Servings

Cabbage cooks especially well in the microwave oven and with minimal odor, too.

CABBAGE IN CREAM SAUCE

**4 cups (½ med. head) shredded
  cabbage
¼ cup light cream
1 teaspoon cornstarch
½ teaspoon salt
⅛ teaspoon nutmeg
1 tablespoon butter or margarine**

1. Combine all ingredients in 1½-quart glass casserole; stir to combine.
2. MICROWAVE, covered, 6 to 8 minutes or until cabbage is desired doneness, stirring once. 5 to 6 Servings

Carrots and onions — always a delightful flavor combination.

CARROTS DELIGHT

**8 medium carrots, cut into strips
1 small onion, sliced
2 tablespoons butter or margarine
1 teaspoon dried parsley flakes
½ teaspoon grated lemon peel
¼ teaspoon salt
Dash pepper**

1. Combine carrots, onion and butter in 1-quart glass casserole.
2. MICROWAVE, covered, 8 to 10 minutes or until carrots are tender. Stir in remaining ingredients.

5 to 6 Servings

TIP • *Variable Power:* Microwave high 5 minutes. Then, microwave low (30%) for 8 to 10 minutes.

This orange and ginger sauce is added after the carrots are tender.

GINGERED CARROTS

8 medium carrots, sliced
2 tablespoons butter or margarine
½ tablespoon sugar
1 teaspoon cornstarch
½ teaspoon salt
¼ teaspoon ground ginger
3 tablespoons orange juice

1. Combine carrots and butter in 1-quart glass casserole.
2. MICROWAVE, covered, 6 to 8 minutes or until just about tender. Combine remaining ingredients; mix until smooth. Stir into carrots.
3. MICROWAVE, covered, 1 to 2 minutes or until mixture boils.

5 to 6 Servings

TIP • *Variable Power:* In step 2, microwave high 4½ minutes. Then, microwave low (30%) 5 to 6 minutes. Complete step 3 as directed.

Sesame seed is toasted similarly to almonds.

CAULIFLOWER WITH TOASTED SESAME SEED

2 tablespoons sesame seed
3 tablespoons butter or margarine
1 small head cauliflower
4 green onions, sliced
¼ teaspoon salt
Dash pepper
1 teaspoon lemon juice

1. Combine sesame seed and butter in 1-quart glass casserole.
2. MICROWAVE, uncovered, 3 to 4 minutes or until seeds are lightly toasted, stirring once. Separate cauliflower into flowerettes; slice ¼ inch thick. Add to casserole along with onions.
3. MICROWAVE, covered, 5 to 7 minutes or until cauliflower is tender. Sprinkle with salt, pepper and lemon juice; toss lightly to season evenly.

4 to 5 Servings

TIP • If butter spatters in step 2, place a paper towel over casserole.

Butter provides the moisture for cooking fresh cauliflower.

COMPANY CAULIFLOWER

1 small head cauliflower
2 tablespoons butter or margarine
½ cup grated Parmesan cheese
1 teaspoon dill weed
¼ teaspoon garlic salt
¼ teaspoon salt

1. Separate cauliflower into flowerettes. Combine with butter in 1-quart glass casserole.
2. MICROWAVE, covered, 7 to 9 minutes or until cauliflower is tender. Combine remaining ingredients; sprinkle over cauliflower. Toss lightly to season evenly. Cover and let stand a few minutes before serving.

4 to 5 Servings

TIP • Cauliflower can be left whole; cook in step 2 for 9 to 11 minutes. Drizzle with butter and sprinkle with cheese mixture.

This method is especially convenient when cooking 6 ears of corn or less.

CORN-ON-THE-COB

1. Remove husk and silk from corn; wash. Arrange ears in shallow casserole. Cover with casserole cover or waxed paper.
2. MICROWAVE until corn is done, rearranging ears once:

2 ears - 3½ to 4½ minutes
4 ears - 7 to   8 minutes
6 ears - 9 to 11 minutes

TIPS • For frozen corn, microwave 2 ears 7 to 9 minutes; microwave 4 ears 11 to 13 minutes.

• The corn husk can replace the covered cooking casserole. Just remove the silk from the corn, wash corn and bring husk back around corn. Microwave as directed for corn-on-the-cob.

Pictured, clockwise: Sour Cream Potato Boats, page 55, Candied Yams, page 56, and Make Ahead Onion Mashed Potatoes, page 56.

This traditionally baked dish is prepared more quickly in the microwave oven. It is cooked uncovered to maintain the crisp crumb topping.

SCALLOPED CORN

    1 can (17 oz.) cream-style corn
    1 can (4 oz.) mushroom pieces,
      drained
    1 egg
    ½ cup soda cracker crumbs
    1 tablespoon chopped chives
    Dash pepper
    ¼ cup soda cracker crumbs
    2 tablespoons butter or margarine

1. Combine corn, mushrooms and egg in 1-quart glass casserole; mix well. Stir in ½ cup crumbs, the chives and pepper. Spread evenly in casserole. Sprinkle with ¼ cup crumbs. Cut butter into pieces and place on top of crumbs.

2. MICROWAVE, uncovered, 8 to 9 minutes or until mixture is set in center. Let stand a few minutes before serving.

4 to 5 Servings

The crumb topping adds a festive finish to these vegetables. Pictured on page 48.

PEAS AND ONIONS

    1 package (10 oz.) frozen peas
    1 package (10 oz.) frozen onions
      in cream sauce
    ¼ teaspoon salt
    ⅛ teaspoon nutmeg
    2 tablespoons butter or margarine
    ¼ cup dry bread crumbs
    ½ teaspoon dried parsley flakes
    2 tablespoons chopped nuts

1. Combine peas and onions in 1½-quart glass casserole.

2. MICROWAVE, covered, 10 to 12 minutes or until hot, stirring once. Stir in salt and nutmeg; set aside.

3. MICROWAVE butter in small glass dish about ½ minute or until melted. Stir in bread crumbs, parsley and nuts. Sprinkle over peas and onions.

4. MICROWAVE, uncovered, 1 to 2 minutes or until hot.   6 to 8 Servings

Carrots are started first since they require more cooking time than peas.

DILLY PEAS AND CARROTS

    4 medium carrots, sliced
    1 tablespoon butter or margarine
    1 package (10 oz.) frozen peas
    ½ teaspoon dill weed
    ¼ teaspoon salt
    Dash pepper

1. Combine carrots and butter in 1 or 1½-quart glass casserole.

2. MICROWAVE, covered, 5 minutes. Add peas.

3. MICROWAVE, covered, 5 to 6 minutes or until carrots are tender. Stir in remaining ingredients.

6 to 8 Servings

POTATO AND SQUASH REMINDERS

• Both potatoes and squash cook faster if left whole and unpeeled. The cooked potatoes or squash will have a steamed texture. If you prefer a more mealy texture to your potatoes, complete them with the browning element or place them in the conventional oven for a few minutes.

• It is not unusual for one side of the potatoes to cook faster than the other. Turning the potatoes over and rearranging part way through cooking helps to even this cooking.

• Potatoes become withered and tough when overcooked. They are best if cooked until they give slightly when pressed. Then let stand 5 to 10 minutes. When ready to serve, microwave 1 to 2 minutes to reheat and complete any necessary cooking.

• With squash, like acorn, leave whole and cook as directed, turning over once or twice. Once cooked, cut the squash in half and scoop out the seeds. If it is necessary to cut the squash in half before cooking, just scoop out the seeds and place squash cut-side-down in glass baking dish. The cooking time will be a little longer than when the squash is left whole.

Use these times for regular white potatoes, sweet potatoes or yams. Use these timings for baked potatoes as well as when cooking potatoes to use in a salad or casserole.

BAKED POTATOES

1. MICROWAVE unpeeled potatoes until they just begin to feel soft, turning potatoes over halfway through cooking time:
  1 medium potato - 4 to 5 min.
  2 medium potatoes - 5 to 6 min.
  4 medium potatoes - 11 to 13 min.
  6 medium potatoes - 15 to 17 min.
  8 medium potatoes - 18 to 20 min.
10 medium potatoes - 22 to 25 min.

2. Let stand 10 minutes.

3. MICROWAVE 1 to 3 minutes or until tender.

TIP • For a drier, more mealy potato, complete with *browning element* for step 3. Brown for 5 to 8 minutes turning potatoes over once. Or, transfer potatoes to a 400° oven for about 10 minutes.

Like oven-fried potatoes, but quickly done in the microwave oven.

ONION-POTATO BAKE

  4 medium potatoes, peeled and sliced
  1 medium onion, sliced
  1 teaspoon salt
  1 teaspoon dried parsley flakes
  Dash pepper
  2 tablespoons butter or margarine
  Paprika

1. Combine potatoes, onion, salt, parsley and pepper in 1 or 1½-quart glass casserole. Dot with butter.

2. MICROWAVE, covered, 10 to 12 minutes or until potatoes are tender, stirring twice. Sprinkle with paprika before serving.   4 to 5 Servings

Our home tester thought these were some of the best microwave-cooked potatoes she had tried.

CRUMB-COATED POTATOES

  3 tablespoons butter or margarine
  6 medium potatoes, peeled
  ½ cup cornflake crumbs
  Salt and pepper

1. MICROWAVE butter in small glass dish ½ to 1 minute or until melted. Dip potatoes into butter, turning to coat; then roll in crumbs. Place in 8-inch square glass baking dish. Sprinkle with salt and pepper. Cover with paper towel.

2. MICROWAVE 16 to 18 minutes or until potatoes are just about tender. Let stand a few minutes before serving.
    6 Servings

These are easy to fix ahead through step 2. Then just heat when ready to serve. Pictured on page 53.

SOUR CREAM POTATO BOATS

  6 medium potatoes
  ⅔ cup sour cream
  2 tablespoons chopped chives
  1 teaspoon salt
  ⅛ teaspoon pepper
  ⅓ to ½ cup milk
  4 tablespoons butter or margarine
  Paprika

1. MICROWAVE potatoes 16 to 18 minutes or until just about tender, turning potatoes over once. Let stand 5 minutes.

2. Cut potatoes in half lengthwise; scoop out insides into mixing bowl, leaving about ¼ inch potato in shell. Mash potato well. Beat in sour cream, chives, salt, pepper and enough milk to make a fluffy consistency. Fill potato shells; place on glass serving plate. Cut butter into 12 pieces; press a piece into top of each potato boat. Sprinkle with paprika.

3. MICROWAVE, uncovered, 3 to 4 minutes or until steaming hot.
    6 to 8 Servings

Use step 1 as a guide for heating the liquid when preparing instant mashed potatoes. Pictured on page 53.

MAKE AHEAD ONION MASHED POTATOES

   2 cups water
   3 tablespoons butter or margarine
   ¾ teaspoon salt
   ⅔ cup milk
   2½ cups instant mashed potato
       flakes
   ½ cup sour cream, if desired
   1 egg
   1 can (3 oz.) French-fried onions

1. MICROWAVE water, butter and salt in covered 1½-quart glass casserole 5 to 6 minutes or until boiling.

2. Stir in milk and potato flakes; let stand a few minutes. Stir in sour cream, egg and half of onions. Spread evenly in casserole. (If desired, let stand several hours at room temperature.)

3. MICROWAVE, covered, 5 to 6 minutes or until heated through. Sprinkle with remaining onions.

4. MICROWAVE, uncovered, 1 to 2 minutes or until hot.   5 to 6 Servings

TIP • When using granular-type potatoes, increase amount to 3 cups.

A fun way to dress up French fries. Pictured on the cover.

EASY CHEESY FRENCH FRIES

   Cheese Sauce, page 65
   1 tablespoon chopped chives
   1 package (16 oz.) frozen
       French fries
   ¼ teaspoon salt

1. Prepare cheese sauce as directed; stir chives into cooked sauce.

2. Place frozen potatoes in 1½-quart glass casserole. Pour cheese sauce over potatoes; sprinkle with salt.

3. MICROWAVE, covered, 8 to 10 minutes or until hot and bubbly, stirring once.   4 to 5 Servings

TIP • For a double amount, use a 2½-quart casserole and microwave 12 to 14 minutes.

The cooking time in step 1 will vary depending upon the size and shape of each potato. Pictured on page 53.

CANDIED YAMS

   6 medium yams or sweet potatoes
   ½ cup packed brown sugar
   ¼ cup butter or margarine
   2 tablespoons orange juice
   ½ teaspoon salt

1. MICROWAVE unpeeled yams 12 to 14 minutes or until tender, turning over once or twice. Let stand 10 minutes.

2. Combine remaining ingredients in 1½ or 2-quart glass casserole.

3. MICROWAVE, uncovered, 3 to 4 minutes or until bubbly and thickened, stirring occasionally.

4. Peel yams and slice into brown sugar mixture; stir carefully to coat yams with mixture.

5. MICROWAVE, uncovered, 7 to 9 minutes or until heated through, stirring once.   6 to 8 Servings

TIP • If desired, add ⅓ cup raisins, ¾ cup drained crushed pineapple or ½ cup whole cranberry sauce in step 4.

A delightful blend of flavors and colors.

SUNSHINE SQUASH

   4 cups (about 1 lb.) sliced winter
       squash
   1 medium apple, peeled and sliced
   2 tablespoons raisins
   2 tablespoons maple or maple-
       flavored syrup
   2 tablespoons butter or margarine
   ½ teaspoon salt

1. Combine all ingredients in 1½-quart glass casserole.

2. MICROWAVE, covered, 10 to 12 minutes or until just about tender, stirring once or twice. Let stand a few minutes before serving. 5 to 6 Servings

WINTER SQUASH WITH BACON

    3 slices bacon
    1 small onion, chopped
    4 cups (about 1 lb.) cubed winter
      squash
    ½ teaspoon salt
    Dash pepper

1. MICROWAVE bacon and onion, uncovered, in 1-quart glass casserole 3 to 4 minutes or until bacon is crisp. Remove bacon; set aside. Add squash, salt and pepper to casserole.
2. MICROWAVE, covered, 10 to 12 minutes or until squash is tender, stirring once. Let stand a few minutes. Crumble bacon and sprinkle over top.

                        4 to 5 Servings

ORANGE-GLAZED ACORN SQUASH

    2 medium acorn squash
    Salt
    2 tablespoons brown sugar
    2 tablespoons butter or margarine
    2 tablespoons raisins
    4 tablespoons orange juice

1. MICROWAVE squash (leave whole) 12 to 14 minutes or until soft, turning once or twice. Let stand 5 minutes.
2. Cut squash in half and scoop out seeds. Place cut-side-up on glass plate. Sprinkle each with salt. Place ½ tablespoon each brown sugar, butter and raisins in each half; add 1 tablespoon orange juice to each.
3. MICROWAVE, uncovered, 4 to 5 minutes or until sauce is bubbly.

                        4 Squash Halves

TIP • For half a recipe, microwave in step 1 for 8 to 10 minutes and in step 3 for 3 to 4 minutes.

ZUCCHINI COMBO

    3 medium zucchini, sliced
      (about 3 cups)
    2 cups (1 pint) sliced fresh
      mushrooms
    1 clove garlic, minced
    2 tablespoons butter or margarine
    2 medium tomatoes, quartered
    ¼ cup grated Parmesan cheese
    Salt and pepper

1. Combine zucchini, mushrooms, garlic and butter in 1½ or 2-quart glass casserole.
2. MICROWAVE, covered, 8 to 10 minutes or until vegetables are tender. Carefully stir in tomatoes. Sprinkle with cheese; season with salt and pepper.
3. MICROWAVE, uncovered, 1 to 2 minutes or until tomatoes are heated.

                        About 6 Servings

BACON-TOPPED TOMATOES

    3 slices bacon
    ⅓ cup dry bread crumbs
    2 tablespoons grated Parmesan
      cheese
    ¼ teaspoon leaf basil
    4 medium tomatoes

1. Arrange bacon in glass baking dish; cover with paper towel.
2. MICROWAVE 2½ to 3 minutes or until crisp. Remove bacon and set aside. Combine 1 tablespoon bacon drippings with crumbs, cheese and basil. Cut tomatoes in half crosswise. Arrange cut-side-up on glass serving plate. Top with crumb mixture; crumble bacon onto each.
3. MICROWAVE, uncovered, 2 to 3 minutes or until tomatoes are warm.

                        4 to 5 Servings

Meal Accompaniments

ABOUT RICE: Rice requires a certain amount of time to soften and become tender. Although microwave cooking cannot speed that time, it can be used for cooking the rice. If rice boils too hard, it tends to boil over. Thus, we slow the cooking by using standing times or a lower power setting.

Quick-cooking rice requires boiling water for rehydrating and this water can be heated in the microwave oven. The longer cooking rice varieties like wild and brown may be more easily cooked on a burner. If you wish to cook them in the microwave oven, use the method for the Fluffy White Rice, but extend the simmer time for the brown rice to about 45 minutes and the wild rice about 60 minutes.

Any type of cooked rice, either refrigerated or frozen, reheats very nicely in the oven. Allow 1 to 2 minutes per cup of rice, and heat right in the serving dish.

This fluffy rice cooks with a minimum of energy. Cook a vegetable or other dish during the standing time.

FLUFFY WHITE RICE

> 1 cup uncooked long-grain rice
> 2 cups water
> 1 teaspoon salt
> 1 teaspoon cooking oil

1. Combine all ingredients in 1½-quart glass casserole.
2. MICROWAVE, covered, 6 to 7 minutes or until mixture boils. Let stand 10 minutes.
3. MICROWAVE, covered, 3 to 4 minutes. Let stand 5 minutes. Fluff with fork and serve.   4 to 5 Servings

TIP • *Variable Power:* Microwave high 6 to 7 minutes or until mixture boils. Then, microwave low (30%) 14 to 16 minutes.

Pictured, top to bottom: Cinnamon-Sugar Muffins, page 63, Hot Cabbage Slaw, page 61, and Noodles Romanoff, page 60.

QUICK-COOKING RICE

> 1¼ cups water
> ½ teaspoon salt
> ½ tablespoon butter or margarine
> 1½ cups quick-cooking rice

1. Combine water, salt and butter in 1-quart glass casserole.
2. MICROWAVE, covered, 3 to 4 minutes or until mixture boils. Stir in rice; cover and let stand 5 minutes. Fluff with fork before serving.
> About 4 Servings

SPANISH RICE

> 6 slices bacon
> 1 cup uncooked long-grain rice
> 1 medium onion, chopped
> ¼ cup chopped green pepper
> 1 can (16 oz.) tomatoes, undrained
> 1 cup water
> ¼ cup catsup
> 1 teaspoon salt
> ½ teaspoon chili powder
> ⅛ teaspoon pepper

1. MICROWAVE bacon, covered with paper towel, in 2-quart glass casserole 4 to 4½ minutes or until crisp. Remove bacon and set aside. Add rice and onion to drippings.
2. MICROWAVE, uncovered, 3 to 4 minutes or until mixture is lightly toasted. Stir in remaining ingredients.
3. MICROWAVE, covered, 7 to 8 minutes or until mixture boils. Let stand 10 minutes.
4. MICROWAVE, covered, 10 to 12 minutes or until rice is tender and liquid absorbed. Crumble bacon and add to rice. Let stand a few minutes before serving.   4 to 5 Servings

TIP • *Variable Power:* In steps 3 and 4, microwave high 7 to 8 minutes or until mixture boils. Then, microwave low (30%) for 20 to 25 minutes.

ABOUT NOODLES: When cooking noodles alone, it is best to use a container on a burner where ample water can be easily used. There are methods of cooking noodles in the microwave oven, but usually no time is saved and it is not possible to use as much water as normal resulting in cooked noodles with a pasty taste and texture.

Once the noodles are cooked, they can easily be reheated with the desired seasonings or sauces in the microwave oven. Also, the oven can be used for any necessary initial cooking of the seasonings or sauce ingredients.

Noodle mixes and a few other recipes that have a sauce with ample liquid, combine the uncooked noodles and the sauce ingredients and these cook together very successfully. Since noodles require a certain amount of time to become tender, the casserole dish must be large enough to allow for the boiling that will take place.

Pictured on page 58.

NOODLES ROMANOFF

        8 ozs. noodles (about 4 cups)
        2 tablespoons butter or margarine
        2 tablespoons all-purpose flour
        1 teaspoon garlic salt
        ¼ cup sliced green onion
        1½ cups milk
        ½ cup sour cream
        ½ cup grated Parmesan cheese

1. Cook noodles as directed on package; drain.
2. MICROWAVE butter in 1½-quart glass casserole about ½ minute or until melted. Stir in flour, garlic salt and onion. Add milk; stir until combined.
3. MICROWAVE, uncovered, 4 to 5 minutes or until mixture boils, stirring occasionally during last half of cooking time. Stir in cooked noodles, sour cream and half of Parmesan cheese. Sprinkle remaining cheese over top.
4. MICROWAVE, uncovered, 3 to 4 minutes or until heated through.

                                    5 to 6 Servings

NOODLES ROMANOFF MIX

        1 package (5.5 oz.) Noodles
          Romanoff mix
        1½ cups water
        ½ cup milk
        2 tablespoons chopped onion
        1 can (4 oz.) mushroom pieces,
          drained

1. Combine noodles and sauce mix with remaining ingredients in 1½-quart glass casserole.
2. MICROWAVE, covered, 10 to 12 minutes or until noodles are just about tender, stirring once or twice. Let stand a few minutes before serving.

                                    4 to 5 Servings

MANICOTTI

        10 manicotti shells
        1 egg, slightly beaten
        2 cups cottage cheese
        ½ cup grated Parmesan cheese
        1 teaspoon dried parsley flakes
        ½ lb. ground beef
        1 small onion, chopped
        1 clove garlic, minced
        1 teaspoon leaf oregano
        1 can (10¾ oz.) condensed
          tomato soup
        ½ cup water
        1 cup shredded Mozzarella
          cheese

1. Cook manicotti shells as directed on package; drain. Combine egg, cottage cheese, Parmesan cheese and parsley. Fill manicotti shells with cheese mixture. Arrange in 12x8 or 13x9-inch glass baking dish; set aside.
2. Crumble ground beef into 1-quart glass casserole; add onion.
3. MICROWAVE, uncovered, 3 to 4 minutes or until meat is set. Break meat into pieces; drain fat. Stir in garlic, oregano, soup and water. Spoon over filled manicotti shells. Cover baking dish with waxed paper.
4. MICROWAVE 10 to 12 minutes or until bubbly throughout. Sprinkle with Mozzarella cheese.
5. MICROWAVE, uncovered, 2 to 3 minutes or until cheese is melted.

                                    6 to 8 Servings

ABOUT SALADS: A few salads require some type of heating or cooking, and most of it is easily accomplished with the microwave oven.

Bacon and potatoes are quickly cooked, a hot or cooked dressing is simple to prepare and liquid is readily heated to dissolve gelatin. Also, some salads that are served warm can be reheated if they cool too much before serving time.

The recipes on this page illustrate some of the uses of the microwave oven in preparing salads. The same techniques can be used for your own favorite salad recipes that require some heating or cooking.

This salad need not be "last minute" with a microwave oven.

GERMAN POTATO SALAD

    5 medium potatoes
    5 slices bacon
    1 medium onion, chopped
    2 tablespoons sugar
    1 tablespoon all-purpose flour
    1 teaspoon instant beef bouillon
    1 teaspoon salt
    Dash pepper
    ¼ cup vinegar
    ½ cup water

1. MICROWAVE potatoes 14 to 16 minutes or until they are somewhat soft when pressed, turning potatoes over once or twice; set aside. Arrange bacon in 2-quart glass casserole. Cover with paper towel.

2. MICROWAVE 3½ to 4½ minutes or until crisp. Remove bacon and set aside; add onion to drippings.

3. MICROWAVE, uncovered, 2 to 3 minutes or until onion is partially cooked. Stir in remaining ingredients.

4. MICROWAVE, uncovered, 3 to 4 minutes or until mixture boils. Slice potatoes into hot mixture; toss lightly to coat potatoes with sauce. Crumble bacon over top. Serve warm.

5 to 6 Servings

TIP • If salad cools before serving, reheat by microwaving 2 to 3 minutes.

The microwave oven is used here to cook the bacon and heat the dressing. Pictured on page 58.

HOT CABBAGE SLAW

    3 slices bacon
    1 tablespoon brown sugar
    1 teaspoon salt
    Dash pepper
    ¼ cup vinegar
    4 cups (½ med. head) shredded
      cabbage
    1 stalk celery, thinly sliced
    2 green onions, sliced
    6 radishes, thinly sliced

1. Arrange bacon in 2-quart glass casserole. Cover with paper towel.

2. MICROWAVE 2 to 3 minutes or until crisp. Remove bacon and set aside. Add remaining ingredients to drippings, tossing to coat evenly.

3. MICROWAVE, uncovered, 2 to 3 minutes or until warm. Crumble bacon and sprinkle over top.   6 to 8 Servings

Use your oven to heat the liquid for any favorite gelatin salad.

ORANGE GELATIN SALAD

    2 cups water
    1 package (6 oz.) orange-flavored
      gelatin
  1½ cups orange juice
    ½ cup sour cream
    1 can (11 oz.) mandarin oranges,
      drained
    1 cup seedless green grapes
    1 banana, sliced

1. MICROWAVE water in large glass mixing bowl 4 to 5 minutes or until boiling.

2. Stir in gelatin until dissolved. Stir in orange juice; cool slightly. Blend in sour cream, beating until smooth. Stir in remaining ingredients. Pour into 5-cup mold. Refrigerate until set, about 4 hours. Unmold onto serving plate.

6 to 8 Servings

ABOUT BREADS: Since breads are very porous, they heat and cook quickly. This also means that there is not enough cooking time for the breads to brown, and that they can easily overcook.

Several types of coatings which add color and flavor can be used on breads that are cooked in the microwave oven. Also, doughs containing spices, brown sugar and molasses make the lack of browning less noticeable.

Breads reheat nicely in the microwave oven. There is a tendency to want to overheat rolls. The surface should feel warm only, as the inside is always hotter. Also, sweet fillings or frostings heat faster than the bread part. Overheated breads have a tough chewy texture and if severly over-heated, will toast and burn on the inside.

Breads should not be covered tightly either when cooking or reheating. If any type of covering is needed, it should be a porous material like a paper towel so that the moisture can escape. When reheating bread items, place them on paper which will absorb the escaping moisture. If placed directly on the oven floor or on a plate, the moisture is trapped between the roll and the non-porous surface causing the roll's crust to become soggy.

Use these times for sweet or dinner rolls, pieces of coffee cake, pancakes or French toast.

HEATING BREAD ITEMS

MICROWAVE on paper towel, napkin or plate until outside feels slightly warm (inside will be warmer):

1 item	— about ¼ minute
2 to 3 items	— ¼ to ½ minute
4 to 5 items	— ½ to 1 minute
6 to 8 items	— 1 to 1½ minutes
1 coffee cake or loaf	— 1 to 1½ minutes

With less than 4 frozen rolls, a rest period is not necessary during the heating. With more than 4 frozen rolls or with a whole coffee cake, the microwave time requires a rest period to allow the heat to reach the center without overcooking the edges.

HEATING FROZEN BREAD ITEMS

MICROWAVE on paper towel, napkin or plate until outside feels warm:

1 item	— ¼ to ½ minute
2 to 3 items	— ½ to 1 minute
4 to 5 items	— 1 to 1¼ minutes*
6 to 8 items	— 1¼ to 1½ minutes*
1 coffee cake or loaf	— 1½ to 2 minutes*

TIP • *Turn oven off for a ½ to 1 minute rest period about halfway through microwave cooking time.

By forming the biscuits into a ring shape, there is no slow-to-cook center.

CARAMEL-ORANGE BISCUIT RING

2 tablespoons butter or margarine
1 teaspoon grated orange peel
¼ cup packed brown sugar
¼ cup orange juice
2 tablespoons raisins
1 can refrigerated biscuits

1. Combine butter, orange peel, brown sugar and orange juice in 8-inch round glass baking dish.

2. MICROWAVE, uncovered, 3 to 3½ minutes or until bubbly and slightly thickened, stirring twice. Sprinkle with raisins.

3. Separate can of biscuits into individual biscuits. Arrange in ring around edge of dish, turning to coat with caramel mixture and overlapping as necessary.

4. MICROWAVE, covered with paper towel, 2½ to 3 minutes or until biscuits are set and no longer doughy, rotating dish once. Invert onto serving plate. Serve warm.   4 to 5 Servings

TIP • *Variable Power:* In step 4, microwave medium-high (70%) 3½ to 4 minutes.

QUICK BREAD REMINDERS

- Use a colorful topping or glaze, or select a dough that contains spices or brown sugar so the lack of browning will not be evident.
- Reduce the leavening by about ⅓ when using your own recipes.
- Nut breads tend to be poorly shaped and overcook on the ends of the loaf unless cooked with a lower power setting. When only a full power setting is available, a combination of bake and microwave is desirable.
- Always use paper napkins, paper towels or paper plates when reheating bread items to prevent a soggy crust.

These muffins are pale until the cinnamon-sugar coating is added — then they look as delicious as they taste. Pictured on page 58.

CINNAMON-SUGAR MUFFINS

  ⅓ **cup butter or margarine**
  ½ **cup sugar**
  1 **egg**
  1 **cup unsifted all-purpose flour**
  1 **teaspoon baking powder**
  ¼ **teaspoon salt**
  ¼ **teaspoon nutmeg**
  ½ **cup milk**
Sugar Coating
  2 **tablespoons butter or margarine**
  3 **tablespoons sugar**
  ½ **teaspoon cinnamon**

1. MICROWAVE butter in glass mixing bowl ¼ to ½ minute or until softened. Blend in sugar; beat in egg. Add remaining ingredients except Sugar Coating; stir just until blended.

2. Spoon into paper-lined microwave muffin cups, filling half full.

3. MICROWAVE, uncovered, 2 to 2½ minutes or until muffins are no longer doughy, rotating pan once.

4. MICROWAVE 2 tablespoons butter in small glass dish ½ to 1 minute or until melted. Dip tops of muffins in butter, then in mixture of sugar and cinnamon. Serve warm.

10 to 12 Muffins

TIP • A topping like this one of butter and cinnamon-sugar is good on other favorite microwaved muffins.

For a nicely shaped, evenly cooked nut bread, use this method which combines microwave cooking and baking.

HONEY-BANANA BREAD

  ½ **cup butter or margarine**
  ½ **cup honey**
  2 **eggs**
  1 **cup (2 med.) mashed ripe banana**
  2 **teaspoons grated orange peel**
  3 **tablespoons orange juice**
  2 **cups unsifted all-purpose flour**
  ½ **teaspoon soda**
  ½ **teaspoon salt**
  ½ **cup chopped nuts or dates**
  1 **tablespoon sugar**
  ¼ **teaspoon cinnamon**

1. MICROWAVE butter in glass mixing bowl about ½ minute or until softened. Blend in honey; beat in eggs, one at a time. Add banana, orange peel and juice, flour, soda, salt and nuts; stir just until combined.

2. Pour into 8x4-inch glass loaf dish, greased on bottom only. Combine sugar and cinnamon; sprinkle over batter.

3. MICROWAVE medium (50%) 16 to 18 minutes or until toothpick inserted in center comes out clean, rotating dish 2 or 3 times. Cool 10 minutes; remove from pan. Cool completely.   1 Loaf

TIP • If you don't have a medium setting, bake the loaf in a preheated 400° oven fo 15 minutes. Then, transfer to microwave oven and microwave high 5 to 6 minutes.

YEAST BREAD REMINDERS

● Most of the time, you will probably prefer baking yeast breads in your regular oven. It is difficult to find a substitute for the nicely browned crust and many doughs tend to be gummy when cooked in the microwave oven.
● Brown and serve rolls are a natural for microwave cooking since initially you only want to cook them without browning. Then when served, you brown them in the regular oven.
● Frozen bread doughs can be thawed very successfully using the method described here. Most of these doughs, though, are best baked in the regular oven.

Make these several weeks ahead for a special dinner. Then just brown when ready to serve.

BROWN AND SERVE ROLLS

1 cup milk
3 tablespoons butter or margarine
3 to 3¼ cups unsifted all-purpose flour
1 package active dry yeast
1 teaspoon salt
¼ cup sugar
1 egg
1 tablespoon butter or margarine
Poppy or sesame seed

1. MICROWAVE milk and 3 tablespoons butter in 2-cup glass measure 1 to 1½ minutes or until very warm (120-130°).
2. Combine 1½ cups flour, the dry yeast, salt and sugar in large mixing bowl. Add warm milk mixture and egg. Beat at medium speed 2 minutes. Stir in remaining 1½ to 1¾ cups flour to form a stiff dough.
3. Cover; let rise in warm place until doubled in size, 1 to 1½ hours.
4. Turn dough onto floured surface; toss to coat with flour. Knead a few times until no longer sticky. Divide into 16 pieces. Shape each into a 3-inch long roll. Place in greased 10x6-inch glass baking dish, forming two rows lengthwise in dish.
5. MICROWAVE 1 tablespoon butter, in small glass dish ¼ to ½ minute or until melted; brush over rolls. Sprinkle with poppy seed.

6. Cover; let rise in warm place until doubled in size, about 30 minutes.
7. MICROWAVE, uncovered, 4½ to 5 minutes or until no longer doughy, rotating dish once or twice. Remove from pan; cool completely.
8. Wrap and refrigerate up to 3 days or freeze up to 3 months.
9. Preheat oven to 425°. Place frozen rolls on baking sheet.
10. BAKE 8 to 10 minutes or until golden brown.   16 Rolls

TIP ● Your microwave oven can be used as a warm place to let the bread rise. Place about 2 cups water in a 2-cup glass measure in oven. Microwave about 4 minutes or until steaming hot. Turn off oven. Place bread dough in oven (no need to cover dough). Close door and allow dough to rise. If the oven becomes cool, just remove the bread dough and turn on the oven to heat the water. Or, with *Variable Power,* place water and bread dough in oven. Microwave warm (10%) 10 minutes; let stand 10 minutes or until doubled in size.

Use this method to thaw frozen bread dough when you need it quickly. The water helps keep the oven warm and prevents overheating the bread.

THAWING FROZEN BREAD DOUGH

1. MICROWAVE 4 cups water in 4-cup glass measure 8 to 10 minutes or until boiling.
2. Place loaf of frozen bread dough in greased 8x4-inch glass or metal loaf pan. Place, uncovered, in microwave oven along with water.
3. MICROWAVE ½ minute. Turn off oven and let bread stand in oven 20 minutes.
4. Repeat step 3 three times. Let bread dough continue to stand in oven until doubled in size, 15 to 30 minutes.
5. BAKE in preheated oven as directed on package.   1 Loaf

TIPS ● For 2 loaves, repeat step 3 four times.
● Use your timer as a reminder for the standing time.

ABOUT SAUCES: Sauces cook from all sides in the microwave oven, eliminating any chance of scorching.

Often a glass measuring cup makes a handy container for measuring, cooking and pouring. Store leftover sauce in a glass jar. Then to reheat, just remove the metal cover and microwave the sauce about 1 minute for each cup of sauce.

Sauces thickened with flour or cornstarch need to come to a boil to cook these thickening agents. Occasional stirring during the last half of cooking is important. This prevents the starches from cooking into a mass that would cause lumps.

Sauces thickened with egg yolks need frequent stirring to prevent the yolks from overcooking near the edge before the center is heated and thickened. Usually these sauces need to become hot, but should not boil.

For ease in stirring, most sauces are cooked uncovered. Covering is more important when using a casserole dish than when using a glass measuring cup. The increased surface on the casserole will require slightly longer cooking times than the measuring cup unless the casserole is covered to hold in the heat.

A favorite holiday sauce, but also good anytime with pork or chicken.

CRANBERRY-ORANGE SAUCE

2 cups cranberries
1 cup sugar
1 tablespoon grated orange peel
½ cup orange juice

1. Combine all ingredients in 1-quart glass casserole.
2. MICROWAVE, covered, 5 to 6 minutes or until cranberries are popped, stirring once. Serve warm or cold. 2 Cups Sauce

Here is an easy way to make gravy.

GRAVY

¼ cup all-purpose flour
1½ cups water or milk
½ cup pan drippings
Salt and pepper

1. Combine flour and water in 4-cup glass measure. Mix until smooth. Stir in drippings.
2. MICROWAVE, uncovered, 3 to 4 minutes or until mixture boils, stirring occasionally during last half of cooking time. Season with salt and pepper. 2 Cups Gravy

An all around basic sauce to dress up many meals.

WHITE SAUCE

2 tablespoons butter or margarine
2 tablespoons all-purpose flour
½ teaspoon salt
Dash pepper
1 cup milk

1. MICROWAVE butter in 2-cup glass measure about ½ minute or until melted. Stir in flour, salt and pepper. Add milk all at once; stir until combined.
2. MICROWAVE, uncovered, 2½ to 3½ minutes or until mixture boils, stirring occasionally during last half of cooking time. 1 Cup Sauce

TIPS • For a double amount, use a 4-cup measure and microwave 5 to 6 minutes.
• CHEESE SAUCE: Add ¼ teaspoon dry mustard with flour and stir ½ to 1 cup shredded cheese into cooked sauce.
• MORNAY SAUCE: Omit salt and add 1 teaspoon instant chicken bouillon with flour; add ¼ cup each grated Parmesan cheese and shredded Swiss cheese to cooked sauce.

Desserts

ABOUT DESSERTS: Many desserts cook beautifully with the microwave oven. Techniques vary depending upon the type of dessert — pudding, fruit, gelatin or cake-type.

Any dessert that normally tastes best served warm is easily reheated with microwaves. Just allow about ¼ minute for each serving being heated.

An old-fashioned favorite that is light, delicious and good for you, too.

TAPIOCA PUDDING

  2 cups milk
¼ **cup sugar**
¼ **cup quick-cooking tapioca**
¼ **teaspoon salt**
  2 eggs, separated
  2 tablespoons sugar
  1 teaspoon vanilla

1. Measure milk into 4-cup glass measure. Add ¼ cup sugar, the tapioca, salt and beaten egg yolks; mix until blended.
2. MICROWAVE, uncovered, 5½ to 6½ minutes or until mixture boils, stirring occasionally during last half of cooking time.
3. Beat egg whites in large bowl until frothy. Gradually add 2 tablespoons sugar, beating until soft peaks form. Fold in vanilla and hot tapioca mixture. Serve warm or cold.   4 to 6 Servings

PUDDING REMINDERS

• Use a 4-cup glass measure for measuring the liquid, cooking the pudding and pouring into the serving dishes.
• Stirring occasionally during the last half of cooking time is important. The thickening ingredients tend to settle to the bottom during the first part of the cooking; if not stirred, they will cook into a mass that will cause lumps. Stirring once or twice as the mixture begins to thicken should be adequate to assure a smooth consistency.
• Cook puddings uncovered for ease in stirring and to prevent the mixture from boiling over.

Pudding is a delight to cook with microwaves — no scorching and no constant stirring.

PUDDING MIX

  2 cups milk
  1 package (4-serving size) pudding and pie filling mix

1. Measure milk into 4-cup glass measure. Add pudding mix; stir to combine.
2. MICROWAVE, uncovered, 5 to 6 minutes or until mixture boils, stirring occasionally during last half of cooking time. Serve warm or cold.
               About 4 Servings

TIP • For 6-serving size pudding mix, use 3 cups milk and microwave 7 to 8 minutes in a 4-cup glass measure.

Pictured: Baked Apples in Butterscotch Sauce, page 69, and Simple Cheesecake, page 72.

CUSTARD REMINDERS

• Keep custard mixtures just below the boiling point. If overcooked, they will curdle and separate.
• Individual custards will cook at different rates. This reflects to some degree the variation in cooking pattern within your oven.
• With custard mixtures that are cooked as one unit, it is easy for the outside to overcook before the center is done. To help even this cooking, use a lower power setting or set the dish of custard in another baking dish with some water. This way, part of the microwaves heat the water and part help cook the custard.

This recipe illustrates how various areas of the oven may cook at different speeds.

INDIVIDUAL BAKED CUSTARDS

    2 cups milk
⅓ cup sugar
    3 eggs
¼ teaspoon salt
    1 teaspoon vanilla
    Nutmeg

1. Measure milk into 4-cup glass measure. Add sugar, eggs, salt and vanilla. Beat with rotary beater until smooth. Pour into five 6-oz. or six 5-oz. glass custard cups. Sprinkle with nutmeg.
2. MICROWAVE, uncovered, 4 to 5½ minutes, removing custards as they begin to bubble. Serve warm or cold.
5 to 6 Servings

TIP • *Variable Power:* Microwave medium (50%) 14 to 16 minutes, rearranging once.

BAKED CUSTARD

1. Prepare mixture for Individual Baked Custards, above. Pour into 1-quart glass casserole; sprinkle with nutmeg. Place casserole in 8-inch square glass baking dish. Add 1 cup warm water to baking dish.
2. MICROWAVE, covered, 8 to 10 minutes or until knife inserted near center comes out clean.
5 to 6 Servings

TIP • *Variable Power:* Microwave medium (50%) 17 to 19 minutes.

This bread pudding received many compliments from the home tester and also when prepared in class.

LEMON 'N RAISIN BREAD PUDDING

¼ cup butter or margarine
    4 slices bread, cubed
⅔ cup sugar
    1 teaspoon grated lemon peel
    2 tablespoons lemon juice
⅓ cup raisins
    1 cup milk
    3 eggs
    Cinnamon

1. MICROWAVE butter in 1-quart glass casserole ½ to 1 minute or until melted.
2. Add bread, sugar, lemon peel and juice and raisins. Toss to thoroughly mix. Combine milk and eggs; beat until smooth. Pour over bread mixture. Sprinkle with cinnamon.
3. Place casserole in 8-inch square glass baking dish. Add 1 cup warm water to baking dish.
4. MICROWAVE, uncovered, 10 to 12 minutes or until center is just about set. Serve warm with light cream.
5 to 6 Servings

TIP • *Variable Power:* Microwave medium (50%) 11 to 13 minutes.

The ingredients here are similar to baked custard, but the stirring keeps it soft. Serve with fresh fruit or over cake or fruit cobblers.

SOFT CUSTARD SAUCE

    2 cups milk
⅓ cup sugar
    1 tablespoon cornstarch
¼ teaspoon salt
    3 eggs
    1 teaspoon vanilla

1. Measure milk into 4-cup glass measure. Add sugar, cornstarch, salt and eggs; beat with rotary beater until smooth.
2. MICROWAVE, uncovered, 4½ to 5½ minutes or until mixture begins to bubble, stirring occasionally during last half of cooking time. Stir in vanilla. Beat until smooth with rotary beater. Serve warm or cold.   2½ Cups Sauce

TIP • *Variable Power:* Microwave medium (50%) 10 to 12 minutes.

FRUIT SAUCE REMINDERS

• Use either water or fruit juice for the liquid. Use only enough liquid to achieve the consistency desired.
• Add sugar before cooking fruit when you wish to retain the shape of the fruit; after cooking when a sauce-like consistency is desired.
• Covering speeds the cooking of fruit sauces.

APPLESAUCE

6 to 8 medium cooking apples, peeled and quartered
½ cup water
½ to ¾ cup sugar
½ teaspoon cinnamon, if desired

1. Combine apples and water in 2-quart glass casserole.
2. MICROWAVE, covered, 9 to 11 minutes or until apples are soft, stirring once. Stir in sugar and cinnamon.   5 to 6 Servings

Our home tester suggested using a melon baller to easily remove the core from the halved apples. Recipe pictured on page 66.

BAKED APPLES IN BUTTERSCOTCH SAUCE

3 medium cooking apples
3 tablespoons brown sugar
½ tablespoon all-purpose flour
2 tablespoons water
1 tablespoon butter or margarine
Cinnamon

1. Cut apples in half lengthwise; remove core, but do not peel. Arrange cut-side-up in 8-inch round glass baking dish. Cover with waxed paper or casserole cover.
2. MICROWAVE 2 to 3 minutes or until apples are just about tender. Combine brown sugar, flour and water; spoon over apples. Dot with butter; sprinkle with cinnamon.
3. MICROWAVE, covered, 2 to 3 minutes or until sauce is bubbly and apples are tender. Serve warm with sauce.   4 to 6 Servings

Orange is the special flavor in this rhubarb sauce. Cornstarch thickens it slightly.

TART AND TANGY RHUBARB SAUCE

4 cups sliced rhubarb
2 tablespoons cornstarch
1 teaspoon grated orange peel
¼ teaspoon nutmeg
1 cup sugar
½ cup orange juice

1. Combine all ingredients in 1½-quart glass casserole.
2. MICROWAVE, covered, 8 to 10 minutes or until mixture boils and thickens, stirring once.
                    4 to 6 Servings

TIP • If using frozen rhubarb, either thaw the rhubarb first, or increase the cooking time to allow for the thawing necessary.

A nice fruit combination to serve plain or over cake.

FRUIT DELIGHT

¼ cup butter or margarine
¼ cup honey
1 teaspoon cornstarch
2 teaspoons grated orange peel
2 tablespoons lemon juice
¼ cup orange juice
1 stick cinnamon
1 can (29 oz.) sliced peaches, drained
1 can (20 oz.) chunk pineapple, drained
¼ cup drained Maraschino cherries

1. Combine all ingredients except peaches, pineapple and cherries in 1½-quart glass casserole.
2. MICROWAVE, uncovered, 3½ to 4½ minutes or until bubbly. Remove cinnamon stick. Carefully stir in peaches, pineapple and cherries.
3. MICROWAVE, covered, 3 to 4 minutes or until heated through. Serve warm or cold with whipped cream or ice cream.   About 6 Servings

CRISP AND COBBLER REMINDERS
• The use of dark brown sugar and spices in the topping enhances the color.
• When additional browning of the topping is desired, use your browning element or place the food under the broiler for a few minutes.
• Toppings become crisper as they cool. The moisture from the warm fruit filling may make them seem quite soft when first removed from the oven.
• Crisps and cobblers are cooked uncovered so that the topping will not become soggy.

This recipe cooks longer than the Apple Crisp recipe because the fruit juices need to boil and thicken in the center of the dish.

RHUBARB CRISP

   5 cups sliced rhubarb
   1 tablespoon all-purpose flour
   ¼ cup honey
   ¼ cup butter or margarine
   ½ cup packed brown sugar
   ½ cup unsifted all-purpose flour
   ½ cup rolled oats
   ½ cup chopped nuts
   ¼ teaspoon cinnamon or nutmeg

1. Combine rhubarb and 1 tablespoon flour in 8-inch square glass baking dish. Drizzle with honey; set aside.
2. MICROWAVE butter in glass mixing bowl ¼ to ½ minute or until softened. Mix in remaining ingredients with fork just until crumbly. Sprinkle over rhubarb.
3. MICROWAVE, uncovered, 15 to 17 minutes or until mixture is bubbly in center.   About 6 Servings

TIPS • Frozen rhubarb can be substituted for fresh. Microwave 3 to 4 minutes or until thawed.
   • *Browning Element:* After microwaving, place crisp 2 inches from element. Brown 10 to 15 minutes, rotating dish once.

Cinnamon adds color and flavor to the topping of this popular favorite.

APPLE CRISP

   6 cups (6 med.) peeled, sliced cooking apples
   1 tablespoon lemon juice
   ⅓ cup butter or margarine
   ¾ cup packed brown sugar
   ½ cup unsifted all-purpose flour
   ½ cup rolled oats
   ½ teaspoon cinnamon or nutmeg

1. Combine apples and lemon juice in 8-inch square glass baking dish; set aside.
2. MICROWAVE butter in glass mixing bowl ¼ to ½ minute or until softened. Mix in remaining ingredients with fork just until crumbly. Sprinkle over apples.
3. MICROWAVE, uncovered, 12 to 14 minutes or until apples are tender.
          About 6 Servings

TIP • *Browning Element:* After microwaving, place crisp 2 inches from element. Brown 10 to 15 minutes, rotating dish once.

A popular share-with-your-neighbor recipe that cooks nicely in the microwave oven, too.

CHERRY CRUNCH COBBLER

   ½ cup butter or margarine
   1 can (21 oz.) prepared cherry pie filling
   1 can (8 oz.) crushed pineapple, undrained
   1 package (9 oz.) yellow cake mix (one-layer size)
   ½ cup chopped nuts

1. MICROWAVE butter in small glass dish about 1 minute or until melted.
2. Combine pie filling and pineapple in 12x8-inch glass baking dish. Sprinkle dry cake mix and nuts over fruit; drizzle with melted butter.
3. MICROWAVE, uncovered, 15 to 17 minutes or until bubbly throughout. Serve warm or cold.   About 8 Servings

TIP • *Browning Element:* After microwaving, place cobbler 2 inches from element. Brown 10 to 15 minutes, rotating dish once.

GELATIN DESSERT REMINDERS

• Unflavored gelatin is first softened in cold liquid, then heated to dissolve completely.

• Flavored gelatin dissolves quickly in boiling water.

• If a gelatin mixture cools too much and becomes firm, just microwave a few seconds or until warmed to the right consistency.

• For gelatin desserts with a soft, mounded appearance, cool the gelatin mixture until partially thickened before folding in the whipped cream or egg whites.

A creamy dessert with gelatin "sparkles". Pictured on the cover.

FRUIT AND CREAM SPARKLE

1 cup water
1 package (3 oz.) favorite flavor gelatin
1 can (17 oz.) fruits for salad
1 cup whipping cream

1. MICROWAVE water in 4-cup glass measure 2 to 3 minutes or until boiling. Stir in gelatin until dissolved. Drain fruits and set aside; add water to liquid to make 1 cup. Stir into gelatin. Pour into 8-inch square pan. Refrigerate until set, 2 to 3 hours.

2. Cut gelatin into ½-inch cubes. Release from pan using a wide spatula. Place about ¾ cup of cubes in 1-cup glass measure.

3. MICROWAVE ¼ to ½ minute or until just about melted. Beat cream until thickened in large mixing bowl. Beat in melted gelatin. Fold in fruits and remaining gelatin cubes. Refrigerate ½ to 1 hour or until mixture thickens. Spoon into serving dishes. Refrigerate until set, 1 to 2 hours.   6 to 8 Servings

TIP • Fruit cocktail can be substituted for fruits for salad.

If you like chocolate pudding, you will love this special-occasion version.

LUSCIOUS CHOCOLATE PUDDING

¼ cup cold water
1 envelope (1 tablespoon) unflavored gelatin
1 cup milk
½ cup sugar
⅛ teaspoon salt
2 squares unsweetened chocolate
3 eggs, separated
⅓ cup sugar
1 teaspoon vanilla
1 cup whipping cream

1. Measure water into 4-cup glass measure. Add gelatin; let stand a few minutes to soften gelatin. Stir in milk, ½ cup sugar, the salt and chocolate.

2. MICROWAVE, uncovered, 4 to 5 minutes or until mixture boils, stirring occasionally. Beat mixture until chocolate is completely melted. Beat in egg yolks. Cool.

3. Beat egg whites until frothy. Gradually add ⅓ cup sugar, beating until soft peaks form. Beat in vanilla. Beat cream in large mixing bowl until thickened. Fold in chocolate and egg white mixtures. If desired, spoon into individual serving dishes. Refrigerate until set.   6 to 8 Servings

A refreshing, creamy dessert that begins with flavored gelatin.

FRUIT BAVARIAN

1 cup water
1 package (3 oz.) raspberry-flavored gelatin
1 pint (2 cups) vanilla ice cream
1 banana, sliced
1 can (8 oz.) crushed pineapple, drained

1. MICROWAVE water in 4-cup glass measure 2 to 3 minutes or until mixture boils. Stir in gelatin until dissolved. Add ice cream; stir until melted. Fold in fruit.

2. Spoon into dishes. Refrigerate at least 2 hours or until set. Serve, topped with whipped cream.

5 to 6 Servings

The microwave oven easily cooks the custard and the blender quickly purées the cottage cheese for this refrigerated cheesecake.

A delicious, creamy-textured cheesecake. Serve plain, or if desired, top with sweetened fruit. Pictured on page 66.

REFRIGERATED CHEESE TORTE

¼ cup butter or margarine
1¼ cups graham cracker crumbs (about 15 squares)
2 tablespoons sugar

Filling
1 cup milk
2 envelopes (2 tablespoons) unflavored gelatin
¾ cup sugar
2 eggs, separated
2 teaspoons grated lemon peel
2 tablespoons lemon juice
2 cups cottage cheese
¼ cup sugar
1 cup whipping cream

1. MICROWAVE butter in 12x8-inch glass baking dish ½ to 1 minute or until melted. Stir in crumbs and 2 tablespoons sugar. Set aside ¼ cup of crumbs; press remaining into bottom of baking dish.

2. Combine milk and gelatin in 4-cup glass measure. Let stand a few minutes to soften gelatin. Blend in ¾ cup sugar and the egg yolks; beat until smooth.

3. MICROWAVE, uncovered, 3 to 3½ minutes or until mixture begins to bubble, stirring once. Stir in lemon peel and juice. Cool about 10 minutes.

4. Combine cottage cheese and custard mixture in blender container. Process at medium speed until cheese is smooth. Beat egg whites until frothy. Gradually add ¼ cup sugar, beating until soft peaks form. Beat cream in large mixing bowl until thickened. Fold in egg white and cheese mixtures. Pour over crumb crust in baking dish. Sprinkle with remaining crumbs. Refrigerate at least 3 hours or until set. Serve cut into squares.   12 to 15 Servings

TIP • If desired, assemble torte in 9-inch spring form pan. Use a glass mixing bowl to combine crust ingredients.

SIMPLE CHEESECAKE

¼ cup butter or margarine
1 cup graham cracker crumbs (about 12 squares)
2 tablespoons sugar

Filling
1 package (8 oz.) cream cheese
⅓ cup sugar
1 egg
1 tablespoon lemon juice

Topping
1 cup sour cream
3 tablespoons sugar

1. MICROWAVE butter in 8-inch round glass baking dish ½ to 1 minute or until melted. Stir in crumbs and sugar. Press over bottom and ½ inch up sides of dish.

2. MICROWAVE cream cheese for Filling in glass mixing bowl ½ to ¾ minute or until softened. Beat in sugar and egg. Blend in lemon juice. Pour into crust.

3. MICROWAVE, uncovered, 2 to 3 minutes or until set around edges, rotating dish once.

4. Combine sour cream and sugar for Topping. Spoon over cheesecake, spreading to cover.

5. MICROWAVE, uncovered, 1 to 1½ minutes or until topping is heated. Cool. Refrigerate until served.
          6 to 8 Servings

TIP • *Variable Power:* In step 2, microwave medium-high (70%) 4 to 5 minutes, rotating dish once. In step 5, microwave medium-high (70%) 1½ to 2 minutes.

CAKE DESSERT REMINDERS
- Rotating the dish once or twice during cooking will help assure an evenly cooked cake.
- Dishes are greased on the bottom only. However, even when the dish is not greased, the dessert still removes easily from the baking dish.
- Cake-type desserts that are normally steamed are cooked covered to hold in the steam and aid the cooking.

This traditional steamed pudding recipe is cooked covered to achieve the steamed effect.

CHRISTMAS PUDDING

 2 cups unsifted all-purpose flour
 1 cup packed brown sugar
 1 teaspoon soda
 1 teaspoon cinnamon
 1 teaspoon nutmeg
 ½ teaspoon salt
 ¼ teaspoon cloves
 1 cup raisins
 1 cup mixed candied fruit
 ½ cup chopped nuts
 1½ cups sliced carrot
 ⅔ cup orange juice
 ½ cup cooking oil
 1 egg

1. Combine all ingredients except carrot, juice, oil and egg in large mixing bowl. Combine carrot, juice, oil and egg in blender container. Process at medium speed until carrot is finely chopped. Add to other ingredients; stir until thoroughly combined.

2. Grease a 2 or 2½-quart glass casserole or mixing bowl. Place a glass 1½ to 2 inches in diameter in center of bowl, open-end-up. Spoon pudding batter around glass, spreading evenly. Cover with plastic wrap.

3. MICROWAVE 9 to 11 minutes or until cake around glass is no longer doughy, rotating dish 2 or 3 times. Let stand, covered, 10 minutes. Remove glass; invert pudding onto serving plate. Serve warm with Butter Sauce or whipped cream.

10 to 12 Servings

TIP • *Variable Power:* Microwave medium (50%) 9 minutes. Rotate dish and microwave high 6½ to 7½ minutes.

Use these times for cooking plain gingerbread, too. The topping makes this recipe extra special.

APPLESAUCE GINGERBREAD

 1 package (14 oz.) gingerbread mix
 1 cup sweetened applesauce
 2 cups thawed whipped topping
 ½ cup sweetened applesauce
 Nutmeg

1. Prepare gingerbread mix as directed on package except reduce water by ½ cup and add 1 cup applesauce. Pour into 8-inch square glass baking dish, greased on bottom only.

2. MICROWAVE, uncovered, 7½ to 8½ minutes or until toothpick inserted near center comes out clean, rotating dish once or twice. Cool.

3. Fold ½ cup applesauce into whipped topping. Spoon over gingerbread, spreading to cover. Sprinkle with nutmeg. Refrigerate until served. 8 to 10 Servings

TIPS • When serving the gingerbread warm, spoon the topping onto each individual serving.
 • Sweetened whipped cream can be used for whipped topping.
 • *Variable Power:* Microwave medium (50%) 6 minutes. Rotate dish and microwave high 4 to 5 minutes.

BUTTER SAUCE

 ¾ cup whipping cream
 ¼ cup milk
 ¾ cup sugar
 ½ cup butter or margarine
 ½ tablespoon cornstarch
 1 teaspoon vanilla

1. Combine cream, milk, sugar, butter and cornstarch in 4-cup glass measure; mix well.

2. MICROWAVE, uncovered, 4 to 5 minutes or until mixture boils, stirring once.

3. MICROWAVE 1 more minute. Stir in vanilla. Serve warm. 2 Cups Sauce

Cakes and Frostings

ABOUT CAKES: Most cakes cook in less than ten minutes so little top browning can be expected. By selecting a batter where browning isn't expected or by topping with a creamy frosting or broiled topping, a cake cooked in the microwave oven can be quite versatile.

Cakes, especially mixes, may be quite uneven on top. They rise higher with microwave cooking, so usually there will be extra batter from a cake mix. The extra can be used to make a few cupcakes. With cakes made from scratch, it is usually advisable to reduce the leavening to about ⅔ of the original amount.

Cakes can be cooked with a high setting. However, the Variable Power method usually is preferred because it produces a cake with a more even top surface and a finer texture. Rotating is important with any cake for evenly cooked results in minimal time.

With some ovens, there is a tendency for cakes to remain doughy in the center of the bottom. If you find this to be a problem, try elevating the cake slightly on an overturned sauce dish. Sometimes this changes the cooking pattern enough to eliminate the problem. Or, heat water in the dish for a few minutes while mixing the cake batter. Then, remove the water and grease the dish. The heat in the dish helps cook the bottom of the cake.

Don't be misled by moist areas on the cake surface, thinking the cake needs additional cooking. This situation happens quite frequently with cake-type products. When you notice this condition, touch it with a finger to see if it is only on the surface or if it extends into the cake. If it is only on the surface, additional cooking normally does not help and it may overcook other areas.

Pictured, top to bottom: Caramel-Topped Oatmeal Cake, page 77, and Fruit Cocktail Cake, page 76.

CAKE MIXES — MICROWAVE METHOD

1. Prepare favorite cake mix batter as directed on package.
2. Pour into 12x8-inch glass baking dish, greased on bottom only. Fill dish only half full (use leftover batter for cupcakes).
3. MICROWAVE, uncovered, 9 to 11 minutes or until toothpick inserted in center comes out clean, rotating dish once or twice. Cool. Frost with favorite frosting.   12x8-inch Cake

TIPS • For round layers, line bottom of two 8-inch round glass baking dishes with waxed paper. Fill dishes half full. Microwave, one dish at a time, 5 to 6 minutes or until toothpick inserted near center comes out clean.

• For 8-inch square layers, prepare as for round layers but use all the batter. Microwave, one dish at a time, 7 to 8 minutes or until toothpick inserted near center comes out clean.

• For a more even crust, allow the cake mix batter to stand in baking dishes about 10 minutes before cooking.

• *Variable Power:* Microwave medium (50%) 8 minutes. Rotate dish and microwave high 4 to 5 minutes.

• *Browning Element:* After Microwaving, place cake 3 inches from element. Brown 10 to 12 minutes, rotating once.

BUNDT-TYPE CAKE

1. Prepare favorite Bundt-type cake mix as directed on package. Lightly oil a 12-cup fluted microwave cake pan; sprinkle with sugar. Pour batter into pan, spreading evenly.
2. MICROWAVE medium (50%) 10 minutes. Rotate dish and Microwave high 5 to 6 minutes or until no longer doughy.   16 to 20 Servings

TIP • If Variable Power is not available, Microwave 11 to 13 minutes, rotating dish every 4 minutes.

CAKE REMINDERS

• The recipes call for greased pans, but in general, with the moist microwave cooking, it is difficult to distinguish if the pan was greased or not. Leave the sides of the pan ungreased so that the cake can cling to it as it rises. Avoid greasing and flouring the pan, as this causes a tough layer on the cake.
• Fill pans only ½ full rather than the usual ⅔ full. This is especially important with mixes that are cooked with all microwave cooking.
• Test cakes in the normal way — with a toothpick or the touch of a finger.
• Check small, moist areas on the surface to see if the cake is not yet done or if it is only moist on the surface.
• Rotate the cake occasionally during cooking to assure a more evenly cooked cake.
• Cake layers may tend to be fragile. Refrigerating a few hours makes handling and frosting much easier.
• Oiling the cake dish and then sprinkling with sugar is recommended for Bundt-type cakes.

A popular favorite that cooks quickly and deliciously in the microwave oven. Pictured on page 74.

FRUIT COCKTAIL CAKE

      1 can (29 oz.) fruit cocktail, drained
      1 cup sugar
      1 egg
   1½ cups unsifted all-purpose flour
      ¾ teaspoon soda
      1 teaspoon salt
      ½ cup chopped nuts
      ¾ cup packed brown sugar

1. Combine fruit, sugar and egg; beat well. Stir in flour, soda and salt, mixing well. Spread in 8-inch square glass baking dish, greased on bottom only. Sprinkle with nuts and brown sugar.
2. MICROWAVE, uncovered, 9 to 10 minutes or until cake is no longer doughy, rotating dish 2 or 3 times. Serve warm, topped with whipped cream or ice cream.

                              8-inch Square Cake

TIP • *Variable Power:* Microwave medium (50%) 7 minutes. Rotate dish and microwave high 7 to 8 minutes.

Normally a loaf cake is difficult to cook with just microwaves because the center takes so much longer to cook than other parts. This fruitcake is an exception because the high sugar content speeds the cooking of the center.

HOLIDAY FRUITCAKE

   1½ cups unsifted all-purpose flour
      ¾ cup packed brown sugar
      ½ teaspoon baking powder
      ½ teaspoon salt
      1 teaspoon cinnamon
      ¼ teaspoon nutmeg
      ¼ teaspoon allspice
      ¼ cup molasses
      ⅓ cup cooking oil
      ½ cup liquid*
      2 eggs
      2 cups (1 lb.) chopped candied fruit
      1 cup chopped dates
      1 cup raisins
      1 cup walnut or pecan halves

1. Combine all dry ingredients in large mixing bowl. Combine molasses, oil, liquid and eggs; mix well. Add to dry ingredients; stir until blended. Stir in remaining ingredients.
2. Line bottom of 9x5 or 8x4-inch glass loaf dish with waxed paper. Spoon fruitcake batter into dish, spreading evenly.
3. MICROWAVE, uncovered, 11 to 13 minutes or until toothpick inserted near center comes out clean, rotating dish occasionally. Cool 15 minutes. Remove from dish; cool completely. Wrap first in brandy or rum-soaked cheesecloth, then in foil. Let stand several weeks before slicing and serving.

                              9 x 5-inch Fruitcake

TIPS • *Use fruit juice such as orange, grape or apple. Or, use half fruit juice and half brandy or rum.

• *Variable Power:* Microwave medium (50%) 12 minutes. Rotate dish and Microwave high 7 to 8 minutes.

This delicious oatmeal cake is topped with a gooey caramel mixture that is also cooked in the microwave oven. Pictured on page 74.

CARAMEL-TOPPED OATMEAL CAKE

> **1 cup rolled oats (quick or old fashioned)**
> **1½ cups water**
> **½ cup butter or margarine**
> **1 cup sugar**
> **1 cup packed brown sugar**
> **2 eggs**
> **1½ cups unsifted all-purpose flour**
> **1 teaspoon soda**
> **1 teaspoon cinnamon**
> **½ teaspoon salt**
> **½ teaspoon nutmeg**
> **Caramel topping, this page**

1. Combine rolled oats and water in glass mixing bowl.

2. MICROWAVE, uncovered, 3 to 4 minutes or until mixture boils, stirring once; set aside.

3. MICROWAVE butter in large glass mixing bowl about ½ minute or until softened. Blend in sugars until well mixed. Beat in eggs. Add flour, soda, cinnamon, salt, nutmeg and oatmeal mixture; stir just until combined.

4. Pour into 12x8-inch glass baking dish, greased on bottom only.

5. MICROWAVE, uncovered, 10 to 12 minutes or until toothpick inserted in center comes out clean, rotating dish once. Prepare topping; spoon over cake, spreading to cover. Cool.

 12x8-inch Cake

TIP • *Variable Power:* Microwave medium (50%) 8 minutes. Rotate dish and Microwave high 6 to 7 minutes.

CARAMEL TOPPING

> **¾ cup packed brown sugar**
> **6 tablespoons butter or margarine**
> **2 tablespoons milk**
> **1 cup flaked coconut**
> **½ cup chopped nuts**

1. Combine all ingredients in 4-cup glass measure.

2. MICROWAVE, uncovered, 3 to 4 minutes or until bubbly and thickened, stirring several times. Spread on warm or cooled cake.

 Frosts 12x8-inch Cake

It is fun to watch these cupcakes cook, despite their irregular shape.

CUPCAKES

1. Prepare favorite cake mix or cake recipe batter. Line microwave muffin pans or custard cups with paper liners. Spoon batter into cups, filling half full.

2. MICROWAVE, uncovered, until toothpick inserted in center comes out clean:

> 1 cupcake — ¼ to ½ minute
> 2 cupcakes — ¾ to 1 minute
> 6 cupcakes — 1½ to 2 minutes

A sweet topping slows the cooking of cake mix and makes the texture fine and delicate, and the surface more even.

PINEAPPLE UPSIDE DOWN CAKE

> **2 tablespoons butter or margarine**
> **¼ cup packed brown sugar**
> **1 can (8 oz.) crushed pineapple, undrained**
> **1 package (9 oz.) yellow cake mix (one-layer size)**

1. MICROWAVE butter in 8-inch square glass baking dish about ½ minute or until melted. Stir in brown sugar and pineapple; spread evenly in bottom of dish.

2. Prepare cake mix as directed on package. Pour over pineapple mixture in pan, spreading to cover.

3. MICROWAVE, uncovered, 9 to 11 minutes or until toothpick inserted near center comes out clean, rotating dish once or twice. Loosen edge of cake; invert onto serving plate. Serve warm or cold. 8-inch Square Cake

TIPS • CHERRY UPSIDE DOWN CAKE: Melt butter in dish as directed, spoon ½ can prepared cherry pie filling over butter, top with cake batter and cook as directed in step 3.

 • *Variable Power:* Microwave medium (50%) 8 minutes. Rotate dish and microwave high 5 to 6 minutes.

A moist spice cake that cooks nicely with just microwaves. The crumb-nut topping adds an attractive finish.

CRUMB-TOPPED SPICE CAKE

     2 cups unsifted all-purpose flour
     1 cup packed brown sugar
     2 teaspoons cinnamon
     1 teaspoon ginger
     ¼ teaspoon salt
     ½ cup shortening
     1 cup buttermilk or sour milk
     2 tablespoons molasses
     ½ teaspoon baking powder
     ½ teaspoon soda
     1 egg
     ¾ cup chopped nuts or flaked
        coconut

1. Combine flour, brown sugar, cinnamon, ginger and salt in large mixing bowl. Cut in shortening until mixture is crumbly. Set aside ½ cup of mixture for topping.

2. Add buttermilk, molasses, baking powder, soda and egg to remaining crumb mixture. Beat until smooth. Pour into 12x8-inch glass baking dish, greased on bottom only. Sprinkle with nuts and reserved crumbs.

3. MICROWAVE, uncovered, 9 to 11 minutes or until toothpick inserted near center comes out clean, rotating dish once. Serve warm or cold.

                    12x8-inch Cake

TIP • *Variable Power:* Microwave medium (50%) 7 minutes. Rotate dish and microwave high 4 to 5 minutes.

A spicy oatmeal coffee cake with its own streusel topping.

STREUSEL COFFEE CAKE

     1 cup unsifted all-purpose flour
     ½ cup rolled oats (quick or
        old fashioned)
     1 cup packed brown sugar
     ½ cup butter or margarine
     ½ teaspoon baking powder
     ¼ teaspoon salt
     ¼ teaspoon soda
     ½ teaspoon cinnamon
     ½ cup buttermilk or sour milk
     2 eggs
     ⅓ cup chopped nuts
     ⅓ cup flaked coconut, if desired

1. Combine flour, rolled oats and brown sugar in large mixing bowl; cut in butter until crumbly. Set aside ½ cup mixture. Add baking powder, salt, soda, cinnamon, buttermilk and eggs to remaining crumb mixture. Mix until combined.

2. Pour batter into 10x6-inch glass baking dish, greased on bottom only. Sprinkle with reserved crumb mixture, nuts and coconut.

3. MICROWAVE, uncovered, 7 to 8 minutes or until toothpick inserted near center comes out clean, rotating dish once or twice.

                10x6-inch Coffee Cake

TIPS • The coconut will not toast during the microwave cooking. If desired, use toasted coconut or toast the coconut before sprinkling on cake.

   • *Variable Power* is not recommended for this cake as it causes the topping to sink into the cake.

This carrot cake has received many compliments. Try it with the Cream Cheese Frosting.

GRANOLA CARROT CAKE

     ½ cup butter or margarine
     ¾ cup packed brown sugar
     2 eggs
     2 cups grated carrot (2 large)
     ¾ cup unsifted all-purpose flour
     ½ teaspoon soda
     ½ teaspoon baking powder
     ½ teaspoon salt
     ½ teaspoon cinnamon
     ½ teaspoon nutmeg
     1 cup granola cereal

1. MICROWAVE butter in glass mixing bowl about ½ minute or until softened. Blend in brown sugar; beat in eggs. Stir in remaining ingredients, mixing until combined. Spread in 8-inch square glass baking dish, greased on bottom only.

2. MICROWAVE, uncovered, 7 to 8 minutes or until toothpick inserted in center comes out clean, rotating dish once or twice. Cool. If desired, frost with Cream Cheese Frosting.

                8-inch Square Cake

TIP • *Variable Power:* Microwave medium (50%) 7 minutes. Rotate dish and microwave high 7 to 8 minutes.

ABOUT FROSTINGS: Microwave cooking can be used for the cooking necessary for most frostings. There are several frosting recipes here and a few other ideas included with the cake recipes.

Since frosting mixtures are high in sugar, they heat very quickly. Occasional stirring is necessary to avoid any concentration of sugar that could otherwise overcook.

These same methods and ideas can be used with other favorite frosting recipes that require some heating or cooking.

Try this frosting on brownies, too.

FUDGY GOOD CHOCOLATE FROSTING

1 cup sugar
⅓ cup butter or margarine
⅓ cup milk
1 cup (6-oz. pkg.) semi-sweet chocolate pieces

1. Combine sugar, butter and milk in medium glass mixing bowl.
2. MICROWAVE, uncovered, 1½ to 2 minutes or until mixture boils, stirring once.
3. MICROWAVE 1 more minute, stirring once. Stir in chocolate pieces. Cool until lukewarm. Beat until creamy and of spreading consistency.
Frosts 12x8-inch Cake

The microwave oven is used here to brown the butter, adding rich flavor and color to the frosting.

BROWNED BUTTER FROSTING

3 tablespoons butter or margarine
1½ cups unsifted powdered sugar
½ teaspoon vanilla
1 to 1½ tablespoons milk

1. MICROWAVE butter in uncovered glass mixing bowl 5 to 6 minutes or until lightly browned.
2. Mix in powdered sugar and vanilla. Beat in milk until of spreading consistency. Frost 8-inch Cake Layer

CREAM CHEESE FROSTING

2 tablespoons butter or margarine
1 package (3 oz.) cream cheese
About 2 cups powdered sugar
½ teaspoon vanilla

1. MICROWAVE butter and cream cheese in glass mixing bowl ¼ to ½ minute or until softened.
2. Beat in powdered sugar and vanilla until of spreading consistency.
Frosts 8-inch Cake Layer

This frosting is like the 7-minute type, but made simpler with corn syrup.

FLUFFY MARSHMALLOW FROSTING

2 egg whites
¼ teaspoon salt
¼ cup sugar
¾ cup light corn syrup
1 teaspoon vanilla

1. Beat egg whites and salt at high speed until frothy. Gradually add sugar, beating until soft peaks form.
2. MICROWAVE syrup in uncovered 1-cup glass measure 1½ to 2 minutes or until syrup boils. Pour syrup in thin stream over egg whites while beating at high speed. Continue beating until frosting is of spreading consistency. Beat in vanilla. Frosts 12x8-inch Cake

Be sure the cooking dish has extra space for a minute of boiling.

BROWN SUGAR FROSTING

⅓ cup butter or margarine
¾ cup packed brown sugar
3 tablespoons milk
1¼ to 1½ cups powdered sugar

1. Combine butter and brown sugar in glass mixing bowl.
2. MICROWAVE, uncovered, 1 to 1½ minutes or until mixture is bubbly, stirring once.
3. MICROWAVE 1 more minute, stirring twice. Stir in milk; cool to lukewarm. Beat in powdered sugar until of spreading consistency.
Frosts 12x8-inch Cake

Cookies and Candies

ABOUT COOKIES: Most bar cookies cook quite well with microwave cooking. Since they are high in sugar, some areas may tend to cook faster than others making it necessary to rotate the baking dish once or twice.

Cookies are like breads and cakes in that an overcooked area becomes toasted and then scorched. This browning, though, will be on the inside and may only be discovered by the smell or when the cookie is broken into pieces.

Individual cookies are sometimes questionable for cooking in the microwave oven. Many doughs do not cook evenly and it is possible to have a cookie that is both doughy and scorched. The dry-textured cookie doughs cook fairly evenly. The best way to learn what doughs cook well in the oven is to try a few cookies when you are baking a batch in your regular oven.

Since glass cookie sheets are not available, either a piece of waxed paper or a plastic microwave baking sheet will suffice for cookies. For ease in transferring the cookies on waxed paper to and from the oven, cut a piece of cardboard slightly smaller than the oven and slip it under the waxed paper. Since the microwaves are not affected by the paper, it can remain in the oven during cooking.

INDIVIDUAL COOKIE REMINDERS

• Cookies do not brown on the outside. When done, the moist doughy appearance will have changed to a dry appearance.
• Use doughs where browning is not expected, or roll dough in nuts or cinnamon-sugar before baking. The cooked cookies can also be frosted or sprinkled with powdered sugar.

Pictured, clockwise: Sugar and Spice Nuts, page 85, Basic Sugar Cookies, this page, and Graham-Chocolate Treats, page 83.

• If some cookies cook faster than others, rotate the cardboard and paper once. If some are still cooked before others, remove the cooked cookies by tearing the waxed paper.
• The cookies will be quite soft when removed from the oven. Allow them to cool a few minutes so the waxed paper can be peeled off easily.

This sugar cookie cooks quite evenly. Decorator sugars or icings can add a festive touch.

BASIC SUGAR COOKIES

1 cup butter or margarine
1 cup sugar
1 egg
2 tablespoons milk
1 teaspoon vanilla
3 cups unsifted all-purpose flour
½ teaspoon baking powder
¼ teaspoon salt

1. MICROWAVE butter in large glass mixing bowl about 1 minute or until softened. Blend in sugar; beat in egg, milk and vanilla. Stir in remaining ingredients.
2. Form dough into 1-inch balls. Place balls 2 inches apart on waxed paper. Flatten slightly using fingers, fork or bottom of a glass dipped in sugar.
3. MICROWAVE, uncovered, until cookies no longer appear doughy:
    12 cookies — 2½ to 3 minutes
    8 cookies — 2 to 2½ minutes
Cool a few minutes before removing from paper.   About 40 Cookies

TIPS • For variety add one or more of the following: ½ cup chopped nuts, 1 cup semi-sweet chocolate pieces, 1 cup raisins, 1 cup halved candied cherries.

• For cinnamon-sugar coated cookies, roll balls of dough in mixture of 2 tablespoons sugar and 2 teaspoons cinnamon before placing on waxed paper in step 2.
• *Variable Power:* Use a medium-high (70%) setting. For 12 cookies, cook 3½ to 4 minutes and for 8 cookies use 3 to 3½ minutes.

BAR COOKIE REMINDERS

- Bars will not brown on the outside, but they will overcook on the inside and can eventually scorch in areas.
- Rotating the baking dish once or twice may be necessary to assure even cooking.
- Greasing of the baking dish is optional. Most bars come out of the dish quite easily whether dish is greased or not.
- Since there is no browning to judge doneness, see if the bars are set by pressing with a finger, or in the cake-like bars, use a toothpick. Sometimes the surface will remain moist looking, but the bar is set. If this is the case, further cooking may overcook the interior leaving the moist-looking surface unchanged.
- Don't attempt to double recipes for bars unless you plan to cook the amounts separately. Larger quantities in one baking dish are more likely to overcook in the corners before the center is cooked.

Use these same times and techniques for cooking regular brownies.

PEANUT BUTTER BROWNIES

- **¼ cup butter or margarine**
- **2 squares or envelopes unsweetened chocolate**
- **⅓ cup peanut butter**
- **1 cup sugar**
- **2 eggs**
- **½ cup unsifted all-purpose flour**
- **¼ teaspoon baking powder**
- **½ teaspoon salt**
- **½ teaspoon vanilla**

1. MICROWAVE butter and chocolate in large mixing bowl 1 to 2 minutes or until melted. Stir in peanut butter and sugar; beat in eggs. Add remaining ingredients; stir until smooth. Spread in 10x6-inch glass baking dish, greased on bottom only.

2. MICROWAVE, uncovered, 5 to 6 minutes or until toothpick inserted near center comes out clean, rotating dish once or twice. Cool; cut into bars.

About 36 Bars

TIP • *Variable Power:* Microwave medium-high (70%) 6 minutes. Rotate dish and microwave high 1 to 2 minutes.

These traditional favorites are equally good prepared in the microwave oven. Watch the timing carefully as overcooking makes the corners "crunchy".

DREAM BARS

- **½ cup butter or margarine**
- **½ cup packed brown sugar**
- **1½ cups unsifted all-purpose flour**
- **3 eggs**
- **1½ cups packed brown sugar**
- **3 tablespoons all-purpose flour**
- **½ teaspoon baking powder**
- **¼ teaspoon salt**
- **1 teaspoon vanilla**
- **1½ cups flaked or shredded coconut**
- **½ cup chopped nuts**

1. MICROWAVE butter in glass mixing bowl about ½ minute or until softened. Blend in ½ cup brown sugar and 1½ cups flour until crumbly. Press into bottom of 12x8-inch glass baking dish.

2. MICROWAVE, uncovered, 4 to 5 minutes or until puffed, rotating dish once.

3. Beat eggs until foamy in glass bowl. Beat in 1½ cups brown sugar. Blend in 3 tablespoons flour, the baking powder, salt and vanilla. Stir in coconut and nuts.

4. MICROWAVE 3½ to 4 minutes or until bubbly, stirring once or twice. Pour over crust, spreading to cover evenly.

5. MICROWAVE, uncovered, 5 to 6 minutes or until topping is set (it may still appear moist), rotating dish once or twice. About 36 Bars

TIPS • *Variable Power:* In Step 5, microwave medium-high (70%) 8 minutes. Rotate dish and microwave high 1 to 2 minutes.

• *Browning Element:* After microwaving, place bars 2 inches from element. Brown 8 to 10 minutes, rotating dish once.

PINEAPPLE-DATE BARS

**1 can (8 oz.) crushed pineapple,
undrained**
1 cup chopped dates
2 tablespoons sugar
1 tablespoon all-purpose flour
½ cup chopped nuts
½ cup butter or margarine
¾ cup packed brown sugar
1 cup unsifted all-purpose flour
1 cup rolled oats
½ teaspoon cinnamon
¼ teaspoon salt

1. Combine pineapple, dates, sugar and 1 tablespoon flour in glass mixing bowl.

2. MICROWAVE, uncovered, 3 to 4 minutes or until mixture boils and thickens, stirring once. Stir in nuts; set aside.

3. MICROWAVE butter in glass mixing bowl about ½ minute or until softened. Blend in brown sugar. Add remaining ingredients; mix just until crumbly.

4. Press ⅔ of crumb mixture into greased 8-inch square glass baking dish. Spread date mixture evenly over crumbs. Sprinkle with remaining crumbs.

5. MICROWAVE, uncovered, 7 to 8 minutes or until topping no longer appears doughy, rotating dish once or twice. About 36 Bars

TIP • *Variable Power:* Microwave medium-high (70%) 7 minutes. Rotate dish and microwave high 3 to 4 minutes.

Brownie mix is cooked in the same way as a favorite brownie recipe. However, the mix may be slightly more irregular on top and the edges may cook faster.

BROWNIE MIX

1. Prepare a 22½-oz. package brownie mix as directed on package. Add chopped nuts if desired. Spread in 12x8-inch glass baking dish, greased on bottom only.

2. MICROWAVE, uncovered, 8 to 9 minutes or until brownies no longer appear moist. Cool. About 48 Bars

TIP • *Variable Power:* Microwave medium-high (70%) 6 minutes. Rotate dish and microwave high 4 to 5 minutes.

Our home tester commented that these were nice because they were not as rich as the traditional layered bars. Pictured on page 80.

GRAHAM-CHOCOLATE TREATS

**1½ cups graham cracker crumbs
(about 18 squares)**
**1 can (14 oz.) sweetened
condensed milk**
**1 cup (6-oz. pkg.) semi-sweet
chocolate or butterscotch
pieces**
1 cup chopped nuts

1. Combine all ingredients; spread in greased 8-inch square glass baking dish.

2. MICROWAVE, uncovered, 6½ to 7½ minutes or until center is puffed and top has a dry appearance, rotating dish once or twice. Cool about 1 hour. Cut into squares. About 24 Bars

TIP • *Variable Power:* Microwave medium-high (70%) 6 minutes. Rotate dish and microwave high 1½ to 2½ minutes.

Chocolate pieces and nuts tend to sink to the bottom in bars, so here we sprinkle some of them on the top.

CHOCOLATE CHIP BARS

⅓ cup butter or margarine
1 cup packed brown sugar
2 eggs
1 teaspoon vanilla
1 cup unsifted all-purpose flour
¼ teaspoon baking powder
½ teaspoon salt
½ cup chopped nuts
**½ cup semi-sweet chocolate
pieces**

1. MICROWAVE butter in large glass mixing bowl about 1 minute or until melted. Stir in brown sugar; beat in eggs and vanilla. Stir in flour, baking powder, salt and half each of nuts and chocolate pieces. Spread in 8-inch square glass baking dish, greased on bottom only. Sprinkle with remaining nuts and chocolate pieces.

2. MICROWAVE, uncovered, 5 to 6 minutes or until toothpick inserted near center comes out clean, rotating dish once or twice. About 24 Bars

TIP • *Variable Power:* Microwave medium-high (70%) 7 minutes. Rotate dish and microwave high 1 to 2 minutes.

ABOUT CANDIES: The microwave oven can be used to easily heat or cook mixtures for candies. Since the cooking comes from all sides, there is little chance of scorching.

Some candies use candy-like ingredients that are heated until they can be combined easily with other ingredients. Caramels, marshmallows and chocolate are often used in this way.

Other candies require that a sugar mixture cooks long enough to dissolve. Sometimes this means several minutes of boiling. Be sure a large enough container is used to provide adequate space for the boiling.

More traditional candies are cooked until a certain temperature is reached. Although no recipes of this type are included here, these can be cooked in the microwave oven. However, since most candy thermometers are not made for microwave oven use, the mixture must be removed from the oven when the temperature is checked. Also, since these mixtures become very hot, be sure to use a type of glass cooking container that can tolerate high cooking temperatures.

Children will love to make these easy snacks. Help them with the timing, though, because marshmallows heat quickly and scorch on the inside if overheated.

S'MORES

1. Sandwich 1 square milk chocolate candy and 1 marshmallow between 2 graham cracker squares. Wrap in paper towel or napkin to hold in place.
2. MICROWAVE just until marshmallow softens:
     1 S'more — ¼ to ½ minute
     3 S'mores — ½ to 1 minute
     6 S'mores — 1 to 1½ minutes
Let stand a minute or two to allow chocolate to finish melting.

   TIP • MINT S'MORES: Substitute a chocolate covered mint patty for marshmallow and chocolate.

Chocolate melts quickly and easily in the microwave oven. Just give it a quick stir about halfway through the cooking time to assure that a thin corner does not overcook.

ROCKY ROAD CANDY

   **8 ozs. milk chocolate candy, broken into pieces
   2 cups miniature marshmallows
   ½ cup chopped nuts**

1. MICROWAVE chocolate in large glass mixing bowl 1 to 1½ minutes or until softened, stirring once.
2. Stir in marshmallows and nuts just until coated with chocolate. Spread in buttered 8-inch square pan. Refrigerate 1 hour. Cut into squares.
                    About 36 Pieces

Peanut butter and graham crackers add extra nutrition to these yummy candies.

GRAHAM CRACKER TOFFEE

   **About 14 graham cracker squares
   ¼ cup peanut butter
   ½ cup butter or margarine
   ¾ cup packed brown sugar
   ½ cup semi-sweet chocolate pieces**

1. Spread half of graham cracker squares with peanut butter. Top each with another square and arrange in layer in buttered 8-inch square glass baking dish (break some squares in half).
2. Combine butter and brown sugar in 4-cup glass measure.
3. MICROWAVE, uncovered, 1½ to 1¾ minutes or until mixture boils, stirring once.
4. MICROWAVE 1 more minute, stirring twice. Pour over graham cracker squares; sprinkle with chocolate pieces.
5. MICROWAVE ¾ to 1 minute or until mixture is bubbly and chocolate is softened. Spread or swirl chocolate over top. Cool. Refrigerate about 1 hour. Cut into squares.
                    About 4 Dozen Pieces

CANDY REMINDERS

- If the mixture needs to boil, be sure the container has extra room for the boiling.
- Do not use a regular candy thermometer in the oven as the microwaves can make it inaccurate.
- Since candies are high in sugar, they can scorch or burn if not watched carefully and occasionally stirred.

With a candy like this one that requires several minutes boiling time, be sure there is ample room in the dish for the boiling.

SMOOTH AND CREAMY FUDGE

3 cups sugar
½ cup butter or margarine
1 can (5.3 oz.) evaporated milk (⅔ cup)
2 cups (12-oz. pkg.) semi-sweet chocolate pieces
1 jar (7 oz.) marshmallow creme
1 cup chopped nuts
1 teaspoon vanilla

1. Combine sugar, butter and evaporated milk in 3-quart glass casserole or bowl.
2. MICROWAVE, uncovered, 5½ to 6½ minutes or until mixture comes to a boil, stirring once or twice.
3. MICROWAVE, uncovered, 3 more minutes, stirring occasionally. If necessary, occasionally stop cooking to prevent mixture from boiling over.
4. Stir in chocolate pieces until melted. Blend in remaining ingredients. Pour into buttered 13x9-inch pan. Refrigerate 2 hours; cut into squares.

8 to 9 Dozen Squares

TIPS • This fudge freezes well; just wrap tightly and freeze up to 3 months.

• For ease in removing marshmallow creme from jar, remove most of mixture and then microwave remaining mixture ¼ to ½ minute or until warm. Remove, using rubber scraper.

These sugar and spice-coated nuts toast beautifully in the microwave oven. Our home tester tried them on ice cream and said they were delicious. Pictured on page 80.

SUGAR AND SPICE NUTS

1 tablespoon egg white
2 cups pecan or walnut halves
¼ cup packed brown sugar
1 teaspoon cinnamon

1. Combine egg white and nuts in bowl; mix until nuts are moistened. Combine brown sugar and cinnamon; add to nuts. Mix until well coated. Place in greased 9-inch glass pie plate.
2. MICROWAVE, uncovered, 3½ to 4½ minutes or until coating loses its gloss, stirring occasionally.

2 Cups Nuts

Make these crunchy balls with either popcorn or cereal, or a combination of the two.

POPCORN BALLS

¼ cup butter or margarine
5 cups miniature or 50 large marshmallows
6 cups popped popcorn

1. Combine butter and marshmallows in large glass mixing bowl.
2. MICROWAVE, uncovered, 2 to 2½ minutes or until melted, stirring once. Stir in popcorn, mixing well. Let stand 10 minutes.
3. Form into balls, buttering hands as necessary to prevent sticking. Let stand 1 to 2 hours or until set.

10 to 12 Balls

TIPS • For colored balls, add desired food coloring to melted marshmallow mixture before adding popcorn.

• CEREAL BALLS: Substitute 5 cups favorite ready-to-eat cereal (non-sugared type) for popped popcorn.

Pies

ABOUT PIES: Pies cook very nicely in the microwave oven. However, some types need the crust precooked before the filling is added. Where this is not possible, it is best to complete the cooking with a browning element or in a regular oven in order to make the crust crisp and flaky. Otherwise, the moisture from the filling prevents the crust, especially the bottom, from having this texture.

When both the crust and filling require cooking, it is helpful to partially cook the filling as well as precook the crust. In this way, the final time is shortened and the chances of overcooking the edges lessened.

For precooking the crust, microwaves are very adequate. Although there is little browning of a crust, it becomes very flaky and tender. This method is especially convenient when you do not wish to heat up your oven for just a pastry shell.

The fillings for cream and gelatin pies are cooked like pudding and gelatin desserts. When the thickening is cornstarch, the mixture is cooked until it boils. Stirring is necessary about ⅔ of the way through the cooking to disperse the starch throughout and prevent lumping. With gelatin-type fillings, the mixture is heated until the gelatin dissolves.

Pieces of fruit pie are easily reheated to a warm, freshly baked temperature just before serving. Just place on serving plates and microwave about ¼ minute for each serving.

CRUST REMINDERS
• Some areas of the crust may cook faster than others. Occasionally rotating the pie plate will help even the cooking.
• As the crust cooks, small areas will begin to brown. If these overcook, they may scorch.

Pictured: Apple Pie, page 88, and Pumpkin Pie, page 89.

This method is really nice in summer when you want a pastry shell for a refreshing chilled pie.

BAKED PASTRY SHELL

1. Prepare pastry for 1-crust pie using pie crust mix or favorite recipe. Roll out on floured cloth-covered surface to circle 1 inch larger than pie plate. Fit into glass pie plate. Fold under edge, forming standing rim; flute. Prick bottom and sides with fork.
2. MICROWAVE, uncovered, 4 to 5 minutes or until crust has a flaky appearance, rotating plate once or twice. Cool. 1 Pastry Shell

TIP • *Browning Element:* After microwaving, place pastry 2 inches from element and brown 5 to 8 minutes, rotating once.

Heating a crumb crust helps it hold together and enhances the toasted flavor.

GRAHAM CRACKER CRUST

   ¼ **cup butter or margarine**
1¼ **cups graham cracker crumbs**
   (about 15 squares)
   2 tablespoons sugar

1. MICROWAVE butter in glass mixing bowl ½ to 1 minute or until melted. Stir in crumbs and sugar until combined. Press mixture into bottom and up sides of 9-inch glass pie plate.
2. MICROWAVE, uncovered, 1½ to 2½ minutes or until heated through, rotating plate once or twice.
9-inch Crust

TIPS • VANILLA WAFER CRUST: Substitute vanilla wafer crumbs for graham cracker crumbs; omit sugar.
• CHOCOLATE WAFER CRUST: Substitute chocolate wafer crumbs (plain or cream-filled wafers) for graham cracker crumbs; decrease butter to 3 tablespoons, omit sugar and decrease microwave time to 1 to 1½ minutes.

FRUIT PIE REMINDERS

• Some fruit pies require both microwave cooking and baking. Microwave cooking quickly heats the filling, then the oven heat quickly browns the crust.
• Be sure top and bottom crust are sealed together well as the filling boils a little harder than normal.
• With lattice-topped pies, use a high-standing fluted rim to contain the bubbly filling.
• Use the timings on this page for your other favorite 2-crust fruit pie recipes.

When the bottom crust is omitted, microwave cooking alone is adequate. A sprinkling of cinnamon adds color to the flaky crust.

DEEP-DISH CHEESE 'N APPLE PIE

  6 cups (6 med.) peeled, sliced
    cooking apples
¾ cup sugar
  1 tablespoon all-purpose flour
  1 teaspoon cinnamon
  2 teaspoons lemon juice
¼ cup raisins
  1 tablespoon butter or margarine
  Pastry for 1-crust pie
½ cup shredded cheese

1. Combine apples, sugar, flour, cinnamon, lemon juice and raisins in 1½-quart glass casserole. Dot with butter.
2. Prepare pastry, adding cheese with flour. Roll out pastry on floured cloth-covered surface to size that will fit top of casserole. Place pastry over apples, folding extra pastry under edge. Flute edge. Cut slit in top. Brush pastry with a little milk; sprinkle with additional sugar and cinnamon.
3. MICROWAVE, uncovered, 10 to 12 minutes or until crust no longer appears doughy.   6 to 8 Servings

TIPS • When using pastry that is already prepared and rolled, sprinkle half of cheese over apples and remaining cheese over pastry during last 2 or 3 minutes cooking time.

   • *Browning Element:* After microwaving, place pie 2 inches from element. Brown 7 to 10 minutes, rotating once.

If you enjoy making pies, try this method of cooking. The results may be some of your best tasting, flakiest-crusted pies. Pictured on page 86.

APPLE PIE

  Pastry for 2-crust pie
  6 cups (6 med.) peeled, sliced
    cooking apples
¾ to 1 cup sugar
  1 tablespoon all-purpose flour
  1 teaspoon cinnamon
  1 tablespoon lemon juice
  2 tablespoons butter or margarine

1. Prepare pastry for 2-crust pie, using pie crust mix or favorite recipe. Roll out half of pastry to fit 9-inch glass pie plate. Line pie plate with pastry; trim crust even with edge of pan. Set aside remaining pastry.
2. Combine apples, sugar, flour, cinnamon and lemon juice. Pile into pastry-lined pie plate; dot with butter.
3. Roll out remaining pastry to circle slightly larger than size of pie plate. Cut slits near center. Moisten edge of bottom crust with water. Place top crust over filling. Fold top edge under bottom crust; pinch together to seal edge.
4. MICROWAVE, uncovered, 7 to 8 minutes or until filling begins to bubble. Meanwhile, preheat oven to 450°.
5. BAKE 12 to 15 minutes or until crust is golden brown.   9-inch Pie

A frozen fruit pie cooks with just microwaves and a browning element. A real time and energy-saver with delicious tasting results.

FROZEN FRUIT PIE

1. Transfer frozen pie from foil pan to a glass pie plate.
2. MICROWAVE, uncovered, 15 to 17 minutes or until filling begins to bubble. Meanwhile, preheat oven to 450°.
3. BAKE 12 to 15 minutes or until crust is golden brown.   9-inch Pie

TIP • *Browning Element:* After microwaving, place pie 3 inches from element. Brown 13 to 15 minutes, rotating once.

CUSTARD PIE REMINDERS

• The crust is precooked before adding custard-type fillings.

• By heating or partially cooking the filling, the final microwave time is reduced.

• Occasional rotating of the pie may be necessary during microwave cooking, to cook the filling evenly.

An old-fashioned favorite cooked a new easy way.

CUSTARD PIE

    4 eggs
    ⅔ cup sugar
    ½ teaspoon salt
    1 teaspoon vanilla
    2¼ cups milk
      9-inch baked pastry shell
      Nutmeg

1. Combine eggs, sugar, salt, vanilla and milk in 2-quart glass mixing bowl; beat until smooth.

2. MICROWAVE, uncovered, 7 to 8 minutes or until mixture begins to thicken. Stir 2 or 3 times. Pour into baked pastry shell (in glass pie plate). Sprinkle with nutmeg.

3. MICROWAVE, uncovered, 1 to 2 minutes or until just about set, rotating once.   9-inch Pie

TIPS • *Variable Power:* In step 3, microwave medium-high (70%) 3 to 4 minutes.

  • *Browning Element:* After microwaving, place pie 3 inches from element, brown 8 to 10 minutes, rotating once.

FROZEN PUMPKIN PIE

1. Transfer frozen pumpkin pie from foil pan to a glass pie plate.

2. MICROWAVE, uncovered, 18 minutes, then microwave medium-high (70%) 10 to 12 minutes or until just about set.   9-inch Pie

TIPS • *Browning Element:* After microwaving, place pie 3 inches from element. Brown 13 to 15 minutes.

  • If Variable Power is not available, microwave pie 13 to 14 minutes. Then transfer to 450° oven and bake 20 to 30 minutes.

Pictured on page 86.

PUMPKIN PIE

    2 eggs
    1 cup packed brown sugar
    1 tablespoon all-purpose flour
    1 teaspoon cinnamon
    ½ teaspoon salt
    ½ teaspoon nutmeg
    ¼ teaspoon ginger
    ⅛ teaspoon allspice or cloves
    1 can (15 oz.) pumpkin
    1 can (13 oz.) evaporated milk
      9-inch baked pastry shell

1. Combine all ingredients except pastry shell in 2-quart glass bowl, beat until smooth.

2. MICROWAVE, uncovered, 8 to 9 minutes or until mixture begins to thicken, stirring 2 or 3 times. Pour into baked pastry shell (in glass pie plate). Spread evenly.

3. MICROWAVE uncovered, 6 to 8 minutes or until knife inserted near center comes out clean.   9-inch Pie

TIP • *Browning Element:* After microwaving, place pie 3 inches from element. Brown 10 to 12 minutes, rotating pie once.

PECAN PIE

    ¼ cup butter or margarine
    1 cup dark corn syrup
    ½ cup sugar
    3 eggs
    1 teaspoon vanilla
    1 cup chopped pecans
      9-inch baked pastry shell

1. Combine butter, corn syrup and sugar in 2-cup glass measure.

2. MICROWAVE 2½ to 3 minutes or until mixture boils. Beat eggs; gradually add in hot syrup mixture. Stir in vanilla and pecans. Pour into pastry shell (in glass pie plate.)

3. MICROWAVE medium (50%) 4½ to 5½ minutes or until just about set.
                    9-inch Pie

TIPS • *Browning Element:* After microwaving, place pie 3 inches from element. Brown 10 to 12 minutes, rotating plate once.

  • If Variable Power is not available, microwave in step 3 for 3 to 4 minutes and then bake at 400° for 10 to 12 minutes.

CREAM PIE REMINDERS

• Measure and cook the filling ingredients in a 4-cup glass measure. This also makes it convenient for pouring the filling into the pastry shell.
• Stirring the filling mixture is important during the last half of cooking when the mixture starts to thicken. The thickening settles to the bottom of the mixture and when not stirred will cook into a mass in the bottom. Then, when the mixture is stirred, the mass breaks into lumps.
• Meringue toppings shrink and become tough from microwave cooking. Either brown the topping by placing under a browning element or baking, or fold the meringue into the hot filling.

This delicious pie begins with pudding and pie filling mix. Gelatin helps hold the shape for cutting and serving.

CHOCOLATE-RUM PIE

9-inch Baked Pastry Shell, page 87
2 cups milk
1 package (4-serving size) chocolate pudding and pie filling mix
1 envelope (1 tablespoon) unflavored gelatin
2 tablespoons rum or 1 teaspoon rum flavoring
1 cup whipping cream
2 tablespoons sugar

1. Prepare pastry shell; cool.
2. Measure milk into 4-cup glass measure. Add pudding mix and gelatin; mix well.
3. MICROWAVE, uncovered, 5 to 6 minutes or until mixture boils, stirring once during last half of cooking time. Stir in rum; cool 5 minutes.
4. Spoon filling into pastry shell; refrigerate. Beat cream until thickened; beat in sugar. Spoon over pie. If desired, garnish with chocolate curls.
9-inch Pie

TIP • If desired, add 1 or 2 sliced bananas to pastry shell before adding filling.

Meringues require dry heat for light browning and gentle cooking. The filling for a meringue pie cooks nicely with microwaves.

LEMON-PINEAPPLE MERINGUE PIE

9-inch Baked Pastry Shell, page 87
1 cup sugar
5 tablespoons cornstarch
1 can (8 oz.) crushed pineapple
3 egg yolks
3 tablespoons butter or margarine
1½ teaspoons grated lemon peel
2 tablespoons lemon juice

Meringue
3 egg whites
¼ teaspoon cream of tartar
⅓ cup sugar

1. Prepare pastry shell; cool.
2. Combine sugar and cornstarch in 4-cup glass measure. Drain pineapple, adding water to liquid to make 1½ cups (set aside pineapple). Add liquid to sugar mixture, stirring until smooth.
3. MICROWAVE, uncovered, 4 to 5 minutes or until mixture boils, stirring occasionally. Beat egg yolks slightly. Stir part of hot mixture into egg yolks. Return to 4-cup measure, mixing well.
4. MICROWAVE, uncovered, 1 minute. Stir in butter, lemon peel and juice and pineapple. Pour into pastry shell.
5. Preheat oven to 400°. Beat egg whites and cream of tartar until frothy. Add sugar gradually, beating until soft peaks form. Spoon meringue onto filling, sealing to edge and spreading to cover filling.
6. BAKE 7 to 9 minutes or until meringue is lightly browned. Cool.
9-inch Pie

TIP • *Browning Element:* Omit baking step; place meringue-topped pie 3 inches from element. Brown 13 to 15 minutes, rotating plate once.

GELATIN PIE REMINDERS

• Unflavored gelatin is first softened in cold liquid, then heated until dissolved. When other thickeners such as cornstarch or egg yolks are also present, the mixture must be heated to near boiling.
• Gelatin can also be used in the form of the sweetened flavored gelatin. Here hot water is used to dissolve the gelatin.
• Marshmallows contain gelatin so can be used to make an easy gelatin filling. They also add sweetness and flavoring to the filling.
• For a pretty mounded filling, allow the filling to set until it begins to hold its shape before spooning into the crust.
• Crumb crusts are nice for gelatin-type pies. Although specific flavors are suggested with each filling here, they can be interchanged to suit your taste. A small portion of the crumbs can be reserved to sprinkle on the finished pie.

A simple to make, special-occasion pie.

BRANDY ALEXANDER PIE

Chocolate Wafer Crust, page 87
30 large or 3 cups miniature
   marshmallows
½ cup milk
2 tablespoons dark crème de
   cocoa
2 tablespoons brandy
1 cup whipping cream, whipped

1. Prepare crust; cool.
2. Combine marshmallows and milk in large glass bowl.
3. MICROWAVE, uncovered, 2 to 3 minutes or until marshmallows are just about melted, stirring once. Stir in crème de cocoa and brandy; refrigerate until mixture begins to thicken.
4. Fold whipped cream into marshmallow mixture. Spoon into crust. Refrigerate at least 2 hours or until set. If desired, garnish with additional chocolate wafer crumbs or whipped cream.   9-inch Pie

A holiday favorite. Use this cooking method for other favorite chiffon-type pies.

EGGNOG PIE

Graham Cracker Crust, page 87
1 cup milk
1 envelope (1 tablespoon)
   unflavored gelatin
⅓ cup sugar
1 tablespoon cornstarch
¼ teaspoon salt
2 eggs, separated
1 teaspoon vanilla
2 tablespoons brandy or rum, or
   1 teaspoon brandy flavoring
¼ cup sugar
¾ cup whipping cream
Nutmeg

1. Prepare crust; cool.
2. Combine milk and gelatin in 2-cup glass measure. Let stand a few minutes to soften gelatin. Blend in ⅓ cup sugar, the cornstarch and salt.
3. MICROWAVE, uncovered, 2½ to 3 minutes or until mixture boils. Beat egg yolks slightly; add some of hot mixture, mixing well. Return all of mixture to glass measure; stir to combine.
4. MICROWAVE, uncovered, ½ to 1 minute or until mixture begins to bubble. Stir in vanilla and brandy. Cool to room temperature.
5. Beat egg whites until frothy; gradually add ¼ cup sugar beating until soft peaks form. Beat cream in large mixing bowl until thickened. Fold in beaten egg whites and cooled pudding mixture. Pour into crust. Sprinkle with nutmeg. Refrigerate 2 hours or until set.   9-inch Pie

Index

SUBSTITUTIONS

1 cup buttermilk =	1 tablespoon vinegar or lemon juice plus milk to make 1 cup
1 tablespoon chopped chives =	1 teaspoon freeze-dried chives
1 tablespoon cornstarch =	2 tablespoons flour
1 clove garlic =	1/8 teaspoon instant minced garlic or garlic powder or 1/2 teaspoon garlic salt
2 tablespoons green pepper =	1 tablespoon dried pepper flakes
1 teaspoon dried leaf herbs =	1/4 teaspoon powdered herbs
1 teaspoon grated lemon peel =	1/2 teaspoon dried lemon peel
1 teaspoon grated orange peel =	1/2 teaspoon dried orange peel
1 small (1/4 cup) onion =	1 tablespoon instant minced onion or onion flakes, 1/4 cup frozen chopped onion or 1 teaspoon onion powder
1 tablespoon snipped parsley =	1 teaspoon dried parsley flakes
1 package active dry yeast =	1 scant tablespoon dry or 1 cake compressed yeast